ADAPTATION
VS
NOVELIZATION
The feminist narrative

ADAPTATION VS NOVELIZATION

The feminist narrative

Dr. Rakesh Rana
Associate Professor
Department of English
Govt. College Kullu.
Himachal Pradesh

ANAMIKA PUBLISHERS & DISTRIBUTORS (P) LTD.
4697/3, 21A, Ansari Road, Daryaganj, New Delhi 110 002
Phones: 011-2328 1655, 011-43708938
E-mail: anamikapublishers@yahoo.co.in

First Published 2022

ISBN 978-93-91524-58-6

PRINTED IN INDIA

Published by Anamika Publishers & Distributors (P) Ltd., 4697/3, 21A, Ansari Road, Daryaganj, New Delhi 110 002. Typeset by Shivani Compuers, Delhi 110093 and Printed at Vikas Computer & Printers, Tronica City, Ghaziabad

"One father is more than hundred schoolmasters"

– Geroge Herbert

Dedicated to
my dear father
Late Sh. Kishan Chand Rana

Contents

Preface

In this book an attempt has been made to understand novel and film as two different mediums and their corresponding shift to one another; novel into film and vice versa. The argument in this book centered round four texts; two novels by Basi Sidhwa and two films by Deepa Mehta respectively, former as a novelist and latter as a film maker. Sidhwa and Mehta seem to act in collaboration. Mehta's film the *Earth* is an adaptation of the novel *Ice-Candy-Man* whereas Sidhwa wrote a novel *Water* based on a film of the same name by the former. The debate on cinematic adaptations, fidelity to the original source, divergence, novelization, stigma of borrowing, sticking to the internal logic, maintaining the 'spirit' of the novel and the film in case of novelization are scrutinized in detail. Next important aspect taken under study was to evaluate the proposed four texts in feminine perspective. Feminism and its all-embracing facets including its origin from stone age, three waves of feminism, voices of great feminists, Sidhwa and Mehta's views in their novels and films especially in the proposed text were also incorporated in the study. Some light is also thrown to highlight the intertextuality of these texts. And the four texts are studied in a feminist approach and finally the film text the *Earth* and the *Water* are put under the lens of feminist film theory.

Dr. Rakesh Rana

Introduction

One of the central objectives of this book is to explore, examine and analyze the feminist perspective of Bapsi Sidhwa's novel *Ice-Candy-Man* (1988) and its adaptation into a film *Earth* (1998) by Deepa Mehta. An added objective of this proposed book is to study the novelization of Mehta's film *Water* (2005) into a novel of the same name (*Water*) by Sidhwa. Novel and films are two very important mediums of expression. Every work of art whether a novel or a film, is encrusted with social, cultural, historical, political and economic milieu in which it is produced. Both novel and film need to be examined with multidimensional perspective namely political, philosophical, psychological and feminist. This book engages in investigating the transformation of a novel into a film and vice versa which entails shifting in medium. For this very reason an emphasis is made to study the dual media; visual and textual and their corresponding shift into one another.

At the outset, it is indispensable to have a glance at the various aspects such as film as an art, adaptation, novelization, feminist perspective in the proposed texts and the examination of film texts under the scanner of feminist film theory. It is understood that the film is the youngest of the arts, yet it claims a very serious consideration as an academic discipline. Like the novel, it presents a narrative depicting characters entangled in the conflicts. Like the drama, the film is a visual, verbal and aural medium presenting life on screen for audience in t he theatre. This study attempts to gauge some characteristics of different media in general and a special attention is given to a particular genre, the filmed–novel. The film *1947: Earth* by Deepa Mehta is an adaptation of Bapsi Sidhwa's novel *Ice-Candy-Man* (1988) whereas the novel *Water* (2006) is novelized version of the film *Water* (2005).

The main thrust in this book is to find out how Sidhwa and Mehta use different media, former using literary medium and latter the visual medium to express their viewpoints about women. Sidhwa weaves magic with the words while Mehta uses the moving images to convey the issue of feminism in the proposed texts. The supplemented objective of this book is to explore and analyze critically the shifting aspect of one medium into another such as the transformation of literary text into a visual text (novel into a film) and vice versa.

This book begins with a brief discussion about its title. The discussion commences with a debate about the title of this book. The important terms used in the title of the book is Adaptation and Novelization which means shifting in medium. Therefore it is important to bring to light the term before proceeding further. Merriam Webster dictionary defines medium as "a means of effecting or conveying something." Similarly Macmillan Dictionary defines it "as a particular type of art as a way of expressing idea or feeling." 'Medium' includes and covers a wide variety of phenomena such as speech, writing, print and broadcasting or relates to certain specific technical forms such as radio, television, newspapers, magazines, books, photographs, paintings or films. It is derived from Latin word 'medium', meaning the middle, midst, center or an intermediate agency. It is a means by which something is accomplished; means of expression, channel of communication, substance or an environment through which something is affected. There are theorists who classify media according to the channels involved such as 'visual', 'auditory' and 'tactile'. Human experience is multisensory. Every medium has certain restrictions and is constrained by the channel it utilizes. An idea can be expressed by using different mediums. Every medium uses different set of frameworks and tools to achieve different experiences. In this book the focus is on two very popular and important mediums; the 'narrative medium' and 'film medium'. Transformation of a novel into a film and vice-versa involves the shifting of medium and the apparent overlapping. Since the two media are marked by different traits hence they belong to separate artistic genera. Though, novel and film do possess number of similarities. The distinguishing traits are an account of the fact that the novel is a linguistic medium and the film is essentially a visual medium. The conventions which govern each medium are conditioned by their origins, modes of production, audiences, censorship issues etc. Therefore it is also necessary to find out the ease and obstacles that a film maker and novelist come across when there is a shift in media.

The important word used in the title that needs some elucidation is 'shifting'. 'Shifting' is a change or transformation from one medium to other. There are plenty of ways to express ideas such as through a poem, novel, short story, drama, film, painting, photograph, music, dance, architecture and even gossip. Every method which expresses an idea comes in the form of a text such as a novel or a film, and every text which expresses an idea does not originate in a vacuum. Most of the texts are inspired by some prior text. In this regard Marshal McLuhan, a pioneer in media study suggests that media plays a vital role in affecting the society not only by the content delivered but also by the characteristics of the media. In his master work, *Understanding*

Media: the Extensions of the Man (1964) Marshal concurs "Written narratives are borrowed from oral tales just as movies are borrowed from books and television from film" (vii).

What he wants to say is that the oral literature influences a written narrative which eventually influences the visual narrative. For him medium is an extension of oneself. The film *Earth* is inspired from prior text, the *Ice-Candy-Man.* It is certainly a case of intertextuality. Word 'intertextuality' is derived from the Latin word 'intertexto' which means to intermingle.

> Intertextuality is a creative means used to signify the multiple ways in which any literary text echoes, or is inescapably linked to other texts, whether by open or covert citations and allusions, or by assimilation of the feature of an earlier text by a later text, or simply by participation in a common stock of literary codes and conventions (Abraham 200).

Both the film and the novel are texts; former a visual and auditory latter a literal text. All literary productions occur because of the existence of some prior text. In this thesis an extensive analysis is made to explore the consequences as a result of intertextuality of one text into another with special emphasis given to the selected texts. Therefore an important issue of intertextuality is also explored in this work as it incorporates the concept of adaptation and novelization as well. A French philosopher and a literary critic, Roland Barthes also advocates similar views. He emphasizes the interdependence of any literary text with the earlier texts. He believes that the work of art is a blend of several literary devices employed and absorbed in transformation of the texts. In his view, he says, "Any text is a new tissue of the past citations. Bits of code, formulae, rhythmic models, fragments of social languages, etc. pass into the text and are redistributed within it, for there is always language before and around the text" (39). He seems to echo the views of Julia Kristeva's argument that authors do not create their texts from their own mind, but rather compile them from the pre-existent texts. Simandan quotes Kristeva as saying: "any text is constructed as a mosaic of quotations; any text is absorption and transformation of another" [Kristeva 1980:66]. She suggests that a literary work is not the product of a single author, but of its relationship to other texts. In fact, Intertextutality facilitates to enlarge the expansion of knowledge. Similar views are voiced by Linda Hucheson who says that if one knows the primary text, he/she always feels its presence reflecting some shadow of the previous work. It advocates that art imitates art. It is difficult to locate the original source of the imitated text.

'Feminist Reading' is another key phrase used in the title. It also requires attention to be understood comprehensively. The focus of study is also to examine the selected texts in a feminist perspective with a distinctive and concrete feminist approach. It would be gainful to have a glance at both the novel and the film.

The Novel

In the present scenario novel and films are two very popular media. Compared to poetry and drama novel is of recent origin. But it is certainly older than film. Film is in fact one of the youngest of arts. Making an argument about the similarities and differences between novel and film, George Bluestone writes:

> Because of its history is longer and its material more refined, the novel is more complex. In approaching the novel-a term we have used thus far with a confidence more apparent than real-we are faced internally with the fluidity of its boundaries and externally with its particular relationship to life. If the film is protean because it has assimilated photography,

> music, dialogue, the dance, the novel is protean because it has assimilated essays, letters, memoirs, histories, religious tracts, and manifestoes (7-8).

However, it is difficult to define novel and trace its history of origin. Many believe that novel was born in the 18th century but there are others who opine that novel has its ancestry much older. In this regard Terry Eagleton, a professor of cultural theory writes: "Because it is hard to say what novel is, it is hard to say when the form first arose. Several authors have been proposed as plausible candidates for the first novelist, among them Miguel de Cervantes and Daniel Defoe; but the game of identifying is always dangerous" (119). Commenting about the definition of novel he further writes:

> The truth is that novel is a genre which resists exact definition. The novel is a mighty melting pot, as mongrel among literary thoroughbreds. There seems to nothing it cannot do. It can investigate a single human consciousness in eight hundred pages. Or it can recount the adventures of an onion, chart the history of family over six generations, or recreate Napoleonic wars (119).

To give a very precise and accurate definition and history of novel's origin is tricky. However, most critics agree that the Novel has its roots in the literary form that we know as romance. Novels are romances which have to cope with the prosaic world of modern civilization. "They retain their romantic heroes and villains, wish-fulfillment and fairy tale endings, but now these things have to work out in terms of sex and property, money and marriage, social mobility and nuclear family" (Eagleton 9). Earlier novels were written about the middle class people. The virgin birth of novel is regarded with epistolary novel *Pamela* (1740) by Samuel

Richardson. But some believe Robinson *Crusoe* (1719) by Daniel Defoe to be a prototype. Besides *Moll Flanders* (1722), John Bunyan's *The Pilgrim's Progress* (1678) and Aphra Behn's *Oroonoko* (1688) also claim to be the contenders for this literary genre. But, Stevan Moore, an American author and eminent literary critic in his book '*The Novel: An Alternative History*' (2010) finds the elements of novel, predating *Pamela, Robinson Crusoe, Moll Flander and Pilgrim's Progress.* There are others who believe that lady Murasaki Shikubu's *Genji Monogatari*, a huge Japanese classic written around 1010 can be regarded as the world's first novel, the first modern novel, the first psychological novel. It has many elements which are found in modern novel such as a central character and large number of major and minor characters, well developed characterization and moreover sequence of events. *The Story of Burnt Njal*, a 13th century Ice Landing fiction and then *The Golden Lotus*, a Chinese novel of Ming Dynasty claims to be the earliest contenders to be the novels. However, whichever is anointed as the pioneer of this new literary expression, it has been growing from strength to strength. But to give a very strict definition of novel is very difficult. To define and classify novel with absolute assurance is not possible. However, E.M. Forster quoting Chevalley's definition of the novel, "une *fiction en prose d'une certain etendue*," adds that he will consider a novel any fictitious prose over 50,000 words. The narrative form, the reasonable length, human aspect and the suspense ingredients comprise some essential elements of the novel.

The Film

A film, as a medium of expression disseminates moving pictures, enacts a story by the sequence of images, embellished by sound and music, creating an illusion of continuity. The optical illusion makes the audience perceive continuous motion. Moving pictures have at least two basic possibilities of narrative representation; to represent motion with one shot and to confront two or more comparable states through combination of shots in sequence. Both the modes exhibit visual and auditive dimensions addressing the spectators with sense of vision and sense of hearing. Film, in general, is a narrative medium, or at least, a medium of many narrative capacities.

'Film studies' as an academic discipline is of recent origin. The last couple of decades have witnessed an increase in academic interest in the fields of visual phenomena such as film and photography. Film theory approaches critically a film as an art. Today film studies exist worldwide as a discipline with specific schools dedicated to it. Many liberal arts colleges and universities have designed courses specifically geared towards film studies. But it was only in the ninety 80s and 90s; the inclusion of women in film studies got institutionalized. Lucy Fischer, a distinguished professor of English and Film Studies at university of Pittsburg stresses about the inclusion of women in the film studies, she puts forth: "Women and Film" encompasses numerous issues, including the histories of female practitioners in the industry; the works they produced; female audiences; female critics, historians, archivists and theorists; and the portrayal of women on the movie screen" (Oxford Bibliographies Online). She emphasized on the inclusivity of women in every sphere of the film discipline. Today film studies exist worldwide as a fully-fledged discipline. In the present scenario film studies have grown to encompass numerous aspects such as teaching its history and growth to influence culture and society. In this proposed book the focus will be primarily on the film theory aspect than on the production aspect. Production is associated with technicalities involved in the film making. Film study gives more emphasis on the theoretical aspect. Richard Dyer, an eminent film scholar is of the opinion that film studies is less concerned with advancing proficiency in film production than it is with exploring the narrative, artistic, cultural, economic, and political implications of the cinema. He emphasizes the need to take into account the socio-cultural, psychological, feminist and politico-economic aspects of the films.

Film as an Art or Not?

At the outset the debate argues that whether the film is an art or not and the relation between literature and films. Film is a collaborative art. Commenting about the importance of relationship between film and literature, Louis D. Gianneetti, a professor Emeritus of English and Film writes in his master piece *Understanding Movies* states:

> Film is more complex medium than the traditional arts because movies synthesize many language systems simultaneously, bombarding the spectator with literally hundreds of symbolic ideas and emotions at the same time. (468)

Film as an art combines drama, literature, popular culture, social sciences, acting, journalism, photography, dance and painting. Films convey meaning to audiences in countless ways, communicating and conveying meanings to their audiences through a unique network of language system and techniques. Film as an art is of serious interest. Early inquiry about film was dominated by the question like whether the Film is an art. Whether a film can be taken as an academic discipline? The great Russian film maker Andrei Tarkovsky, one of the greatest film maker of all times emphatically put cinema in the realm of art saying that the art is a meta-language, with the help of which people try to communicate with one another; to impart information about them and assimilate the experience of others. He puts cinema in the realm of art. Commenting about Tarkovsky and films, V. Renee, a renowned film scholar writes:

> Some may take that for granted, however history tells us that film theorists were anything but unanimous on the true nature of the film-Is it a representation of life? Is it art? Is it meant for the betterment of society? Or the promotion of ideals ? Tarkovsky's spiritual and poetic stance on cinema as an art is not only what makes his work so important, but also what guided him through his filmmaking process...Studying Tarkovsky means studying much more than cinema. (No Film School Web)

The Great artist, Pablo Picasso says that an art is not truth. It is a lie that makes us realize truth, at least the truth that is given us to understand. The artist must know the manner whereby to convince others of truthfulness of his lies. Film too is not a reality. It is certainly a representation of reality. Art takes its birth from imperfection. In a short documentary, Tarkovsky explains how art, and therefore filmmaking, wouldn't exist without the imperfection of life. He is of the opinion that the artist exists because the world is not perfect. Art would be useless if the world were perfect, as man wouldn't look for harmony, but would simply live in it. Art is born out of ill-designed world. Art is an expression of human creative skill and imagination typically in visual form such as painting or sculpture, producing works that are to be appreciated for their emotional power.

But it was the emergence of auteur theory that asserted film as an art. Eminent writer Leo Tolstoy defined Art as a diverse range of human activities and the product of these activities. Rudolf Arheim in his book *Film as Art* (2006) asserts that the film resembles painting, music, literature and dance in this respect. Film holds codes, images, and messages in the same manner as traditional literature possess other devices. But there is no dearth of people who do not regard film as an art. They say that film does nothing but reproduce reality mechanically. But many more scholars refute this charge thoroughly. Ever since its birth, film has become a very important part of our contemporary culture. The birth of films is also very interesting and is worth knowing. It has its origin from the idea of an illusion in motion. British Physicist Peter Mark Roget opines that the illusion of motion was first described as the first step in the development of cinema. The history of film making started form 1890, with the invention of first motion-picture cameras.

> When still pictures began to move, they acquired duration, and the photographer was challenged to deal with that fourth dimension. Temporal organization was demanded in addition to spatial composition. As in the novel, the play, music, or dance, an ordering of events into a beginning, middle, and end was required in even the simplest motion picture whether it took the form of a documentary, an avant-garde work, or, most commonly a fictional story. (Wexman 1)

The first ever movie made was *The Horse in Motion* (1878), created by Eadweard Muybridge (a photographer and an inventor). Muybridge was asked by Leland Stanford (a railroad magnet, California senator, race horse owner, and a founder of Stanford University) to answer a popularly debated question: when a horse trots, do all four hooves leave the ground simultaneously? Muybridge's Stop Motion film made it clear that they do. This was perhaps the beginning of film. Kenneth Lonergan, a famous film scholar asserts that film-making, like any other art, is a very profound means of human communication; beyond the professional pleasure of succeeding or the pains of failing, you do want your film to be seen, to communicate itself to other people. Film as an art goes promptly into the conscience of spectators because seeing is believing. Reflecting in his own novel Joseph Conrad formulates his primary ambition.

> "My task which I am trying to achieve is, by the powers of written word, to make you hear, to make you feel-it is, before all, to make to see." (xiv) Conrad's narratives thus embody (provide a locale for) the transformation in the act of taking place. Conrad's own efforts, he says, are to employ the power of the written word, with their origin in the painstaking craft of writing, in order to make his reader experience the vitality and dynamism of the seen things. (Hammer 174)

Conrad's remarks seem to resonate with the filmic remarks of famous American film director, writer and producer D.W. Griffith, who pioneered film making techniques. Griffith states that the task he was trying to achieve was above all to make you see. Similarly, George Bluestone in his work book *Novels into Films* (1957) conveys similar intention by stating "The two ways of seeing, claiming that 'between the percept of the visual image and the concept of the mental image lies the root difference between the two media"(1). All of them communicate the same idea about the importance of film medium.

The Film Explained

It is now essential to explore and examine the differences and similarities between the ways the images are produced in the two media. No other art penetrates so deeply and directly in human conscience as the film does. It reaches deep down to the feelings and into the dark recesses of our souls. The formation of stories with beginning, middle and an end gave birth to films. The films of 1890's were an under a minute film and till 1927, motion pictures were produced without sound. Advent of sound in the film revolutionised this art. The whole world was stunned to see silent things talking. The discovery of sound produced paradigm changes in the film. Such a discovery was not confined to national boundaries, but spread beyond borders throughout the world. Another film scholar Erwin Panofsky acquaints us about the fundamental implications about the origin of film. He says that the primordial basis of the enjoyment of moving pictures was not an objective interest in a specific subject matter, but the sheer delight in the fact that things move, no matter what things they are.

The idea of moving images is an excitement. It is really a very interesting statement which gives an emphasis about the delight in watching the things move. Watching people eating in a restaurant, playing in the fields, walking in streets does not evoke any excitement. But when we see them moving as images on screen, they cause sensation. This excitement of watching moving image gave birth to films. Elaborating further, Panofsky says that films are originally a product of genuine folk-art. At the beginning of things we find the simple recording of movements, galloping of horses, railroad trains, fire engines, sporting events, street scenes. And these films were originally produced by people who did not claim to be the artist, and were enjoyed by people who did not claim to be artists, and who would have been much offended had anybody called them art-lovers. They were taken by photographers who were anything but "directors," and were performed, when it had come to the making of narrative films, by people who were anything but actors. This was how the new media called film was born which tried to free itself from the theatre. As Susan Sontag an American film maker and a writer observes: "The history of cinema is often treated as the history of emancipation from theatrical models" (24).

In contemporary times researches have shown that young adults spend nearly half of their leisure time watching films and videos. The film has become an integral part of their life. It has established its claim as an art very seriously. Cinema as an art form is barely a century old, but within this short span of time it has taken great strides and encroached upon realms and spaces formerly occupied by other art forms. Every art is associated with socio-cultural, economic, and political milieu of the time in which it is created. These works of art cannot be comprehended as independent creations. Film too is not an exception. Film director, Francesca Chiostry says that like all other contemporary art forms films are also the product of the pressure of the religion, politics and the market forces.

The film made out of the novel and vice versa, created long back, in a new political, social, economic set up from that of the original work is a new product. In the forthcoming chapters all these issues of transformations from one text to other and vice versa are studied in a feminist perspective. These artistic ventures (Adaptation and Novelization) need to be deliberated as to what exactly is suggested by these concepts.

Adaptation

Ever since the birth of films, there has been an endless list of novels which inspired them. A film adaptation is the transfer of a written work, in whole or in part, into a feature film. It is a type of derivative work. The most common form of film adaptation is the use of novel as the basis of feature film. It is estimated that one third of the films ever made have been adapted from the novels, and if we include other literary forms such as drama and short stories, that estimate jumps to sixty five percent. Besides being a very popular mode of film making inspired from the novels, there is also an educational angle to films. "There is also an educational reason for adapting literature into film; in this respect, film is pedagogical medium that teaches the masses about their literary heritage" (Desmond and Hawkes 15).

However, the focus of the present study is to understand what happens to popular text such as novels and films when they are transformed into entirely different medium with special emphasis on the selected texts. The basic interest of the field of film and literature is to find how stories travel from medium to medium. Novel is written by an individual author whereas a film is a collaborative effort of a director, dialogue writer and the artists. Novelist enjoys a certain degree of freedom whereas a screenwriter or a director cannot, novelist can ramble on while a screenwriter cannot. The screen writer does not enjoy writing exquisite sentences adorned by similes, metaphors and alliterations. He has to write dialogues within certain time constraint. He envies' novelists for their freedom. Screen writer has to write in box with rigid sides. Despite all this, film has the potential to grab the attention of an entire nation at a same moment in a given time. Not a single book can do this wonder in a particular point of time. This is powerful phenomena associated with films and is considerably rare in the book world. Beside, writing a novel is a lonely affair whereas screen writing involves discussions and meetings. The film accompanies with it many elements.

The film is a mass medium, catering to the needs and interests of vast spectrum of audience from the unlettered to cogno-scenti, and even though it is conceptualized through the vision of individual director, the quality and the depth of final product depends on the versatility of actors who play the particular roles, ingenuity of camera person, editors, choreographer and list of the other factors, including the budget. A film is essentially a collaborative medium. (Asaduddin and Ghosh xv)

Adaptation: Indian Scenario

In India the phenomenon of adaptation is also as old as the birth of cinema itself. The cinema was inspired by mythology and legendary stories. The adaptation of literary text into films is not new phenomenon for Indian film industry. In fact, the first full length feature film of Indian Cinema was based on the life of Raja Harishchandera, a mythological story. It was in the year 1913, *Raja Harishchandera* was released. It was directed by D.G.Phalke, often called "the father of Indian film". He was inspired to make a film about the Indian religious pantheon after viewing a western religious epic. "Could we, the sons of India, ever be able to see Indian images on the screen?' he recalled thinking at a time. Writing about *Raja Harishchandera,* Virginia Wright Wexman puts forth: "*Raja Harishchandera* became the first in a long line of Indian films that drew on Indian mythology for their subject matter" (293).Since then there has been no looking back. The Indian film-makers have directly or indirectly taken references from various literary sources. They were inspired not only by mythological stories but also by the great classics. Writers like Rabindernath Tagore, Bankim Chandra Chatterji, R.K.Narayan, Munshi Prem Chand, and Amrita Pritam were also adapted by film makers. Many of Satyajit Ray's films were made from Bengali and Hindi novels. Decades of 1960s and 1970s witnessed adaptation of Gulshan Nanda's novels into films such as *Kati Patang* (1970), *Neel Kamal* (1968) *and Sharmilee* (1971). Some of the other films which are inspired from novels worth mentioning are: *Pather Panchali* (1955), *Sahib Bibi aur Ghulam* (1962), *Choker Bali* (2003), *Umrao Jaan* (1981),*Pinjar* (2003) etc. Interestingly, most of the earlier films which were made by filmmakers have women at the center. "In 1956 at Cannes, *Pather Panchali* was voted the "best human document" (Wexman 292). Ray is among very few Indian film-makers who have portrayed women characters not of perfect virtues but very real with their fallibility and flaws. He was a filmmaker who understood and portrayed his women characters very deeply. Ray once remarked that he thought to have perhaps a subconscious conviction about women-that they are basically more honest, more forthright because physically they are weaker sex; there are perhaps certain compensating factors in the general makeup of their characters. *Pather Panchali's* Sarbajaya is a woman who finds her life a series of endless hardships. *Pather Panchali* which is an adaptation of Bibhutibhushan Bandopadhyay's novel of the same name is worth mentioning. *Charulata* (1964) is another film made by Ray which deserves to be mentioned. It is an adaptation based on the novella *Nastanirh* (The Broken Nest) by Rabinderanath Tagore. *Charulata* is a very subtle and delicate work. The visual elegance and fluidity of Ray is evident in this film. It is a story of a woman's romantic yearning in the late nineteenth century, pre-independence India. Charulata (Madhabi Mukherjee) trapped in brocaded cage of her house, trying to amuse herself, is a story of a woman establishing her own voice. *Charulata* is Ray's masterpiece about the forbidden love in the late nineteenth century. In 1965 when it was screened at Berlin Film Festival, it won the Silver Bear Award for the best director. Eulogizing Ray for his art of characterization, Phillip Camp observes: "It is not for his technique that one admires Ray so much: no enumeration of gems of *mise-en-scene* would convey the richness of characterization and that breathless grace and radiance he manages to draw from his actors" (criterion.com). Another film worth mention is *Saheb Bibi aur Ghulam,* produced by Guru Dutt and directed by Abrar Alvi is based on a Bengali novel, *Shaheb Bibi Aur Ghulam* (1962) by Bimal Mitra. Commenting about the film and its director Guru Dutt, Virginia Wright Wexman writes that he was a transitional figure in the move toward a progressive Indian art cinema. He was sometimes called the Douglas Sirk of India. He wrote, acted and directed his movies. He represented the plight of the woman in his movies. His film *Saheb Bibi aur Ghulam*(1962)explores the platonic friendship between a beautiful lonely wife (Bibi) of an aristocratic (Saheb) and a part time servant (Ghulam).The film was a huge success and Meena Kumari's performance as Chotti Bahu is regarded one of the best performances in Hindi Cinema. *Umrao Jaan*(1981), a Bollywood film directed by Muzzaffar Ali, inspired from the novel *Umrao Jaan Ada* (1905), written by Mirza Hadi Ruswa, *Parineeta* (1953) produced by Ashok Kumar and directed by Bimal Roy adapted from the novel *Parineeta*(1914) *by* Sharat Chandra Chattopadhya, *Chokerbali* (2003) directed by Rituparno Ghosh based on *Choker Bali* by Tagore and *Pinjar* (2003) directed by Chandra Prakash Dwivedi based on Amrita Pritam's novel *Pinjar* (1950) are some important films inspired from literary sources worth mentioning because all of them deal with the issue of feminism in many forms, like the central theme taken in this proposed work.UmraoJaan (Rekha) like Ayah of *Earth* suffers at the hands of patriarchy.

Feminism in *Ice-Candy-Man* and *Earth*: A Discussion

After discussing in detail about the linkages between the two media the focus shifts in incorporating the feminist aspect of the selected texts. Feminism and cinema are two sets of practices which are interlinked with each other. In this regard Annette Kuhn writes, "The linking of feminism with cinema in itself raises a series of questions, some of them analytical or theoretical, others more obviously political" (3). Linking an issue of feminism to the texts taken into consideration involves social, political, cultural, psychological and economic aspects.

However, the central question which is to be addressed in this book is: what is, can be, or should be the relationship between adaptation, novelization and feminism in context with Bapsi Sidhwa's *Ice-Candy-Man* and *Water* and Deepa Mehta's *Earth* and *Water*. It is interesting to see and examine how the theme of feminism is addressed by employing different narrative media; novel and film. In present day scenario, novels and films are two most popular mediums. Conveying her views about this linkage between the novel and the film, Imelda Whelhan writes:

> Studying both fictional and filming sources can be fraught with problems – particularly in making decisions about giving the 'appropriate amount of attention to each medium, and fostering the skills specific to each form; but perhaps the chief problem lies in teasing out our own and others' conscious and unconscious prejudices about this kind of 'hybrid' study. (3)

Despite adopting different modes of expressions, novelist and the director share a common intention, both want to leave an impact on audience. However, films and novels do magic with different tools. The film is a visual-verbal medium presented before a theatre audience. A novel on the other hand usually presents narrative depicting characters in a series of conflicts. The moment one abandons the linguistics for the visual medium or vice versa, a mutation is inevitable. The metamorphosis of the novel into a film and vice versa is associated with the changing modes of relationship between the two concepts. As for the sake of convenience these differing modes are reduced by an American film theorist, Dudely Andrew to borrowing, intersection, and fidelity. All these three aspects of adaptation will be taken under consideration during the course of this book and an attempt is made to understand both adaptation and novelization from their origin, their fidelity concerns, the advantages and disadvantages the two concepts are associated with and the corresponding changes when they are transformed into one another. Since the texts taken under study are hued in Indian socio-cultural and political milieu. Some light is thrown on the Indian scenario.

Novelization

Novelization, another literary phenomenon taken under study, is not so common a literary phenomenon as is adaptation. The transformation of a film into a novel is called novelization. It is an uncommon literary venture. In this book both these artistic ventures are discussed extensively with a flexible approach to address wide variety of things not just the fidelity concerns.

A Novelization is to put a film into the form of a novel. Unlike adaptation, novelization is rarer activity. One such example is *Water* (2006), the novel written by Bapsi Sidhwa. It has been inspired from Deepa Mehta's film *Water* (2005).Turning of a film into a novel is an unusual choice. It is a big task to translate visual images from a screen into print. Turning a film into a novel might suggest that the film needs to say a lot more than it could have said.

Novelization started in the second half of 1920s when silent films were tuned into the novels. During that time it was easy and profitable to re-experience a popular film. The novelization of the film *Star Wars* (1977) and *Alien* (1979), sold millions of copies. They can reconnect to the experience they enjoyed in watching the film. Novelization requires novelist to multiply approximately 20000-25000 words of the film into at least 60000 words. Hence one important feature of novelization is to increase the volume of pages. This is done by expanding description of incidents and characters. A deep introspection is made into the mind of characters. Sometimes the 'novelizer' invents new scenes to give the plot new dimensions. Most of the 'novelizers' are accomplished writers. They are also the admirers of the film makers.

But there are critics who regard novelization as a "hatch-work". But the central question which is to be addressed in this work is: what is, can be, or should be the affiliation between adaptation and novelization within feminist perspective in the proposed texts. It is interesting to see and examine how Bapsi Sidhwa's women characters are transformed by Deepa Mehta and vice versa. Both Mehta and Sidhwa share their views while representing women. Sidhwa uses a narrative medium while Deepa uses a visual and auditive medium to give an expression to their ideas. But both the filmic and fictional sources are fraught with problems which are also taken into consideration in the present thesis. In this thesis elaborative contrasts and comparisons are also made between the two mediums. As different media have different peculiar properties the results obtained are also different. Bluestone believes that film is based on the optical principle known as persistence of vision. Camera plays a very vital role in visual media i.e. film, it can go anywhere, see anything, in the natural world. Similarly, V.I. Pudovkin, a renowned film scholar says that the lens of the camera replaces the eye of the observer. But there is no brain behind the lens of the camera. It acts an eye for the director without the brain. Differentiating the two, Basil Wright observes that one can look at a crowd and see nothing but an umbrella, or one can look at empty field and see millions of separate blades of grass.... Not so to camera. The lens soullessly records on a sensitized piece of celluloid simply the amount of light of differing values that passes through it. No amount of thinking on the part of the camera man will achieve any other emphasis. Out of a wide landscape it will not pick out that certain tree. Perception of eye and camera are different, former with some bias whereas latter doesn't have any. This difference in perception results in difference in evaluation as well.

Novel as Opposed to Film

Reading of a novel and watching a film are two different experiences. Both these aspects are studied in the later chapters. Film is more sensory experience than reading a novel. Film uses color, sound, movement beside verbal language and light to have desired effect and mood. Light and shadow play a vital role in the film. Consequently, to understand a film requires understanding all these elements. Visual images directly stimulate our perceptions in the film, while written words do it indirectly. Reading the word table requires a kind of mental 'translation' while viewing the table does not. Film is limited by time constraint, while there is no time constraint in a novel. Film has to compress sixty thousand words into two hours or so. The novel involves only one person, the novelist himself, whereas the film is the collaborative effort of large number of people such as screen-writer, director, cinematographer, the actors and technological tools. Novel does provide the freedom to readers to have an interaction with the characters. The readers have full freedom to imagine the characters and can have an imaginary conversation by pausing, while film does not offer this freedom to the viewers. They have to keep pace with the speed of the film. John Howard Lawson believes that the light pattern is the key to the composition, which is never static. The composition is merely a commentary on the action and there is a changing dynamic relationship between each person or object in the scene and camera.

Ever since the birth of films, novels have been providing fodder for them. Borrowing is the most frequently used mode of adaptation. Here the film maker or novelist employs, more or less the same idea or form of an earlier text, generally the one which has already attained some success. Here the film maker sticks to subject and the theme contained in the novel. However, the success of this sort of adaptation rests on the issue of their fertility, not their fidelity. The adapter always hopes to win an audience by the prestige of the borrowed work. This mode of adaptation because of frequent reappearances claims the status of a myth. All great films ever produced are borrowed from books. There is an endless list of the films which are inspired from the novels. Some of the great feminist films inspired and adapted from the novels are: *Birth of a Nation* (1915), the best silent film; *Gone With the Wind* (1939), the best sound film and the best of "all time film", originally both were borrowed from novels. Films like *David Copperfield* (1969), *The Good Earth* (1937), *Wuthering Heights (1992), Pride and Prejudice* (1940), *Lost Horizon* (1973), *Moby Dick* (1956) *etc.* are borrowed from novels. But the vital point is to find out whether the issue of borrowing is important or the result it produces?In this thesis an attempt has been made to uncover this issue in the proposed texts.

The texts taken in the book are also examined by the concept of 'intersection': James Naremore believes that intersection is the mode of adaptation which preserves the "uniqueness of the original text to such an extent that it is intentionally left unassimilated in the adaptation" (30). This mode of adaptation presents otherness and distinctiveness of the original text be it a film or a novel. But the most complex and frequent debate about adaptation is about fidelity and transformation. Fidelity refers to the degree to which a novel or a film retains originality as intended by the novelist or a film maker. The important question is to know the parameters of faithfulness or fidelity associated with the proposed texts. Does it mean to capture the original or to capture its spirit? Both these issues are studied in the chapter I and II with special emphasis on the selected texts. The problems of originality and fidelity are of paramount importance. Conveying his views in this regard, Naremore states that the notion of fidelity of an adaptation certainly contains some degree of truth. Unfaithful presentation of the original work gives some sense of disappointment to both readers and audiences. The words such as infidelity, betrayal, distortion, mutation, violation, vulgarization and desecration become inevitable. Elucidating further he says, 'The notion of fidelity is highly problematic for a number of reasons. First, it is questionable whether strict fidelity is even possible. A counter-view would insist that an adaptation is automatically different and original due to change of medium" (55).

But the moot point is: Fidelity to what? Does it mean that film maker should stick to every detail in the plot? All filmmakers have to condense the novel to his time limit. How could a filmmaker be faithful to the novelist's intentions? Bluestone believes that film maker is an independent artist not a translator of an established author, but a new author in his own right. He also believes that the literal translation is often too foolish. The film maker has to refashion the spirit of story with his or her own vision and tools when the medium is changed. Besides, the contemporary audience or readers want to have narrative suiting their present needs. It demands certain changes. Both novel and film have their own tools for a particular narrative structure. The point he wants to stress on is that audience or the reader must trust the tale not the teller. Most of the commentaries about literary adaptations are formalistic, giving too much emphasis to the textual aspect, explaining the consequences which happen when there is a shift in media. All these concerns are studied in detail in the later chapters.

Now some attention is given to media's specificity of the novel and film. The novel is a single-track verbal medium which has only words to play with whereas a film is multi-track. Film medium is endowed with multi-aspects such as written material, moving photographic image, phonetic sound, music and noises whereas the novel has a single material of expression. The films are endowed with greater resources as compared to novels. Brilliant use of musical instruments is used to create suitable background. The use of natural sounds like the birds singing and the whistling of breeze bring rhythm in telling the story and at that very moment the image on the screen is filled with plethora of details, each carrying multitude information.

Credit must be given to novelists for doing a lot with so little. But we cannot dismiss the film makers for doing so little with so much because of the sheer complexity of this medium. Film's multi-track nature enables it to stage contradictions between image and music which on the contrary a novel lacks. This is a huge advantage that film enjoys. Expressing his views about the advantages, Naremore puts forth:"Although the novelistic character is a verbal artifact, constructed quite literally out of words, the cinematic character is a uncanny amalgam of photo genie, body movement, acting style, and grain of voice, all amplified and molded by lighting, *mis-en-scene*, and music" (60). The advantages and disadvantages each medium is endowed with are illuminated with special reference given to the selected texts.

Another advantage a film enjoys over the novel is that the former has both character as well as performer whereas the latter has only characters. Films are the product of many individuals working together. Myriad names are involved in the making of a film. To coin a phrase, it takes a village to make a movie. Whereas writing of novel involves writer only. It might therefore seem surprising that there is a significant tendency among film scholars to treat films as the product of a single individual, its *auteur* or author. On this line of interpretation, the director of the film is the creative intelligence who shapes the entire film.

Then there is an element of post synchronization in the film. An advantage in having character as well as performer is that the cinema enjoys another entity denied to the novels. In India, playback singers put their voice on the lips of stars on the image tracks. The films, *Earth* and *Water*, both have songs. This makes filmmakers to show the emotional set up through which the character is going through in a more authentic way. Music in itself is very expressive source. In the later chapters the element of sound and music will also be discussed with special reference to the films *Water* and *Earth*.

But films do have some limitations too. They are bound to the budget constraints. Novels are usually written by single author. However, at occasions, novels can be co-authored. The creation of novel is unaffected by the cost constraints. There are novels which are written on napkins in the prisons. The humorous and satirical, *Don Quixote* (1605) is considered to be the first modern European novel is written by Miguel de Cervantes while in prison. Novel can sell 20000 copies and can make substantial profit whereas the film must reach millions. The tools required to write a novel are meager, whereas film calls for an assortment of paraphernalia which needs deep pockets. For hiring actors, equipment and material infrastructure, millions of dollars are required. For making a film, considerable amount of money is required. Three hundred million dollars were spent to make the world's most expensive movie. *Pirates of the Caribbean: At World's End* (2007), followed by movies like *Tangled* (2013), *Spiderman* (2002), *Avatar* (2009), *Harry Potter* (2009) and *King Kong* (2005) etc. Novelist requires almost nothing but a pen. Film requires an elaborate apparatus of studios. The structure of the film is conditioned by budget limits. While dealing with the selected four texts, budget aspect will also be considered. Film *Water,* too was marred by budget constraint. Ajay Virmani, the financer of the film pulled out of the project when Hindu fundamentalists objected to the production of the film. This aspect is also touched upon in chapter III.

Thereafter in this book comparisons are made between the literary tropes such as hyperbole, irony, litotes, metaphor, simile, metonymy, oxymoron, personification, pun, synecdoche and zeugma with somewhat restricted cinematic troupes such as frames, shots, scenes, segue (a short piece of music between two scenes), re-touch (to add details or conceal imperfections on photographic or video image), sequence, editing and masking etc. with special reference to *Ice-Candy-Man* and *Water*(the novels) and *Earth* and *Water* (the films).

Though film adaptation is an accepted phenomenon but there are writers like Virginia Woolf, D.H. Lawrence who are averse to adaptation of their novels into films. Virginia Woolf, contrasting the novel and film says that we must avoid transformation of words into images. She is of the opinion that whenever a literal image is metamorphosed into visual image the disaster is inevitable. She believes that the eye and brain are torn asunder ruthlessly as they try vainly to work in couples. Such type of conversion from linguistic to visual images is disastrous to both. Film commentators like Michael Orme and Thomas Craven also express the similar views that it is very tricky to transpose any one character from page to screen and hope to present him entirely as the novelist created him.

Role of Time in Film and Novel

'Time' plays an important role in visual media especially in films than in novels. The adapter has to compress voluminous novels into a film of two to three hours. It's a mammoth challenge the film maker has to cope with. There are no temporal or spatial constraints while reading a novel. The reader has the choice to set his pace. He can start, stop, re-start, reflect, pause, and go hurriedly wherever he wants. He can enjoy the rhyme and rhythm of the language. A film critic and a script writer, Linda Seger, contrasting two modes of expression, writes that on reading a novel one can see only what the narrator shows us at that particular moment. If the narrator puts the focus in those pages, then we follow the action. If the narrator talks about feelings, then the focus is on the feelings. We can receive only one piece of information at a time. A novel can only give this information sequentially. But film is multidimensional. A good scene in a film advances the action, reveals character, explores the theme, and builds an image. In a novel one scene or an entire chapter may concentrate on only one of those areas. Bluestone expresses similar views as he opines that the novel affords to be voluminous whereas the film is restricted to time constraint. Commenting about the two he writes:

> Further, because of its beholding allows stops and starts, thumbing back, skipping, flipping ahead, and so lets the reader set his own pace, a novel can afford diffusiveness where film must economize. Where the mode of beholding in the novel allows the reader to control his rate, the film viewer is bound by the relentless rate of a projector which he cannot control. (50)

Role of Speed in the Film and the Novel

'Speed' is another important aspect which plays an important role in the film. Novelist takes time to weave a plot and introduce his characters. He dwells in detail and devotes hundreds of pages to introduce the locale and characters whereas a film maker takes fifteen to twenty minutes in eponymous films. Film maker has to go through the process of elimination and attenuation because of the time limit. All the four selected texts are subject to scrutiny in the following chapters.

Censorship Issue

Censorship is another constraint the film is subjected to. The official and unofficial censorship (production code) curtail freedom of a film and constrains it within certain boundaries. But such censorship is not pertinent to novels. The censorship issue haunts filmmakers throughout the world. Governments, film certification departments, religious groups, political groups etc. do impose certain censorship. Not only in India but it's a worldwide phenomena. This issue is also addressed in the later chapter because Deepa Mehta also has to face the problem of censorship in her all major film projects such as *Fire* (1996) and *Water* (2005) *and Earth* (1998).

Presumptions and Predictions in the Novel and Film

While reading a text whether a film, novel, drama or even a painting we start making certain predictions about the content, the message, the title, the audience, aim and so on. And we do this by making inferences from the evidences which we come across. In case of film we may focus on the cover of the DVD's, or trailer, promotion, or the opening of the film. Key points to study film as a text are such as Freeze-Frame, shots-in sequence or sound and image. Tools are used to guess what might happen next, or how the film might end. We may predict what kind of film it might be, what we think about the characters and how things might come to an end.

Element of Sound

Sound is another fundamental element of visual text. Sound,

particularly music, sets the mood of the text as it signifies the genre. It can be more powerful than the visual image. Sound itself carries with it huge amount of narration and information to viewers. Sound helps in interpreting images. Sound-tracks have the elements of music, sound effects, voice and also silence. Sound effects are of two types-atmosphere (continuous sound) or Spot Effects (Short Sounds). In context of sound and image varied number of techniques can be used to develop relationship between them.

Setting, Mood and Question Asking

- Where the film is set? Indoor or outdoor, urban or rural setting?
- When is it set? Day, Night, Morning, Evening, Past, Present, Future?
- Who are in it? Male or female or any other sex, age?
- What are they doing?
- What is happening?
- What is the mood? Tragic or comic? How will it end? Happily or sadly? Beside these the kind of music, speeches, accent and tone etc. are of vital importance. All these issues related to sound and music are discussed in detail.

'Question asking' is another important tool used to read the film. The questions which can be asked generally fall in three categories: literal, inferential and evaluative. During the course of writing as a writer we have to go beyond literal meanings in the film text. Question like how many characters are in the story is a literal one. Where and when the story is set, why a particular character behaved in certain way is an inferential question. What is going through a particular character's mind is also an inferential question. How effectively the director has been able to strike the point he has undertaken is an evaluative question. When we read film as a text subconsciously we make comparisons with the things similar or dissimilar to the text. We take into account things we have read, seen, watched and heard and our own real life experience and sometimes our prior learning is also taken into consideration. We have to ask questions like: Does the present film text reminds me of anything I have read / heard / watched / experienced before. How are they similar? How are they different? Does it remind me of anything in my own life? How would I behave if I were put in the similar circumstances? All these issues are argued in the later chapters.

Role of Lighting in the Film

'Lighting' is another important tool to read a film text. Soft and harsh lighting can manipulate viewer's attitude towards setting or a character. The variegated use of lighting is used to make objects, people and environment look beautiful, ugly soft and harsh or real. Light is used expressively or realistically. For example a heroine is often backlit to create a halo effect and make her look beautiful. Light patterns are important tools used for reading and analyzing a film text. An attempt is made to find patterns in the plot, recurring colours and symbols in both the film texts. Patterns can be found in sound tracks, musical motifs, instruments and sound effects. Sound, image and freeze frames or shots in sequence make the researcher aware of the patterns. The focus is on the things appearing again and again in the film text. Anything we hear more than once in the film. Recurring sound, idea, action, colour, theme, message are given emphasis.

Summarization and Evaluation of Novel and Film

'Summarizing' any piece of work undertaken is an essential skill of a writer. Each piece of information needs to be analyzed and synthesized. Effective summarizing of a film text can be done by making a very effective trailer of the film whether it is a sound only trailer for radio, a poster displaying the would be contents of the film, or selected edits of the shots from the original with appropriate voice over. Summarizing has been taken into consideration such as title of the film, tagline of the film and the pitch of the film which is to be written in less than 25 words.

'Evaluation' is another method used in almost all texts such as a poem, story, novel, drama or a film. Readers in case of written texts and viewers in case of visual text are happy to tell what they feel about the text they have read or seen. But they fail to answer beyond 'Oh!It was a wonderful and exciting or it was boring. The important questions asked in this regard are e.g. what was the author's and director's purpose in making the film based on some novel and vice versa? Did she or he achieve it? What is the filmmaker's or writers' point of view? What about ending? Is it justified? Was this more or less successful as compared to the similar text? This book also attempts to comprehend and analyze all these important points. This study attempts to explore the working of hybrid media. Today, cinema has certainly established itself as a valid medium for communication and has become an instrument of mass culture and entertainment in almost every nook and corner of the world. Now it has definitely attracted the attention of critics and writers to take it more seriously than before. In the present scenario, we see a more harmonious blend of intertextual relation of the two media. In this thesis the argument centers round the transmutation of one text into other and vice-versa i.e. transformation of the novel *Ice-Candy-Man* into the film *1947: Earth* and *Water*, the film into the novel of same name.

After discussing the important aspects with relation to both novel and film, the issue of feminism in the texts of Sidhwa and

Mehta deserves attention. Bapsi Sidhwa and Deepa Mehta is an interesting artistic duo, the former dealing with words while latter with images. Both fall in the category of intellectuals who addressed the issue of feminism with honesty and courage. Sidhwa's novel *Cracking India* and Deepa Mehta's adaptation of it into *1947:Earth* and Mehta's film *Water* and its novelized version are explored and analyzed in the feminist perspective. These works are not only about women but also by women – truly women centered. In an interview about partition, Sidhwa observes that, "at times of such anarchy, women seem to bear the brunt of the attack-they attack a woman because they attacking a man's honour. A woman is often used and misused for these purposes" (changingakistan.wordpress).

Bapsi Sidhwa and Deepa Mehta: A Feminist Author and a Film Maker

Bapsi Sidhwa

Bapsi Sidhwa was born on August 11, 1939 in Karachi, and was brought up in Lahore, then the part of India. Her parents Peshotan and Tehmin Bhandara, belong to an eminent Parsee family which practiced Zoroastrian religion. She was lonely and an isolated child. This put her under serious physical as well psychological limitations. In the early childhood she was struck with polio and went through many surgical operations. The doctor advised her parents not to send her to school. This had a profound effect on her life as it led to loneliness and isolation which left her with no other alternative but to read books. When she came to know that reading books could mitigate her boredom, she took to reading voraciously. She read everything whatever came into her hand and became an avid reader. The first novel she read was *Little Women* (1868) by Louisa May Alcott when she was eleven. She always surrounded herself with books and found in literature the only comfort. Books eased her loneliness during her childhood. She never had chance to go out and play like other children. She made friends from the characters in her books. An Anglo – Indian governess was engaged to take care about her studies at home. At the age of nine she witnessed one of the most poignant events that happened on this blue planet marred by religious intolerance and genocide.

In an interview to Jugnu Mohsin she says that she read some books over and over again. She read *Pickwick Papers* five or six times and P.G Wodehouse was a great favourite with her. From eleven to eighteen she read anything that came her way. She read Russian and American classics. She read Film fare, Femina, comics, P.G Wodehouse, magazines and Pakistani newspaper. She did her matric privately and got her Bachelor of Arts degree from Kinnaird College for women in Lahore. In 1947, when India was cracked, she was just nine years old. She was the witness to communal riots between Muslims on one side and Hindus and Sikhs on the other. She watched it through detached eyes of a child.

She got married to Noshirwan when she was nineteen. It was her second marriage. He was the son of R.K. Sidhwa, a renowned business man and freedom fighter. She is a mother of two girls and a boy. Before becoming a writer she was a housewife and an active social worker. A resilient young woman, she took to writing out of boredom and loneliness. "In an interview to Jugnu Mohsin in the Friday Times of July 20- 26, 1989 Bapsi admitted that as a typical social wife in Lahore, her life was one of unrelieved tedium. She said, "How I abhorred those coffee parties! I tell you, I would've gone mad had it not been my writing" (Dhawan and Kapadia 10-11).

Her first published novel is *The Crow Eaters* but *The Bride* is the first novel she wrote. *The Bride* was rejected by publishers many times. Based on a true story, *The Bride* is about suppression of woman in Pakistani patriarchal society. It is a story of Zaitoon, an obedient Muslim girl married to a tribal man; she rebels at the cruel treatment meted out to her. She escapes from the rigid and traditional society and challenges the structures of patriarchy she is trapped in. In her first published novel *The Crow Eaters*, she gives an account of Parsi life. In this novel she revealed the secrets of Parsi life to the entire world. It is wonderful novel which voices and celebrates the achievements of a tiny community. It describes the social mobility of Parsi Family. Her penetrative insights in presenting the Parsi milieu make *The Crow Eaters* a great entertaining and educative novel. Her novel *Cracking India* was published in 1989 under the title of *Ice-Candy-Man* (1988).This novel shot Sidhwa to international repute. The original title *Ice-Candy-Man* (Meaning Popsicle Vendor) could be mistaken as drug pusher; it was published under the title *Cracking India.* It is her third novel, the most serious political novel. It is her only novel in which she uses a child narrator. This novel examines the inexorable logic of partition as created by communal frenzy at the time of partition. This novel depicts the upheaval which the Hindus, Muslims, Sikhs, Christians and other communities went through. She very subtly delineated the psychological impact of the partition on the lives of people.

Depiction of Lenny as a child narrator struck with polio gives this novel an autobiographical hue. It is novel drawn from personal experience. Eulogizing the novel Robert L. Ross writes: "Cracking India is widely admired in Asia and abroad. It was named by New York Times notable book for 1991. During the same year it received Germany's Literature Award, a prize given to non-European woman writer"(Ross 186).She was Pakistan's only recognized international novelist. It was this novel which inspired Deepa Mehta to make the film *Earth* (1998). After that she wrote a novel, *An American Brat* (1994). This novel examines a very contentious issue amongst the Parsis, the tradition of prohibition of marriage to non-Parsi. It chronicles the adventures of young Pakistani Parsi girl, Firoza Ginwalla in America.

Sidhwa wrote in English, though she is very fluent in several languages such as English, Urdu, Gujrati and Punjabi. Like many sub-continental writers she has no compunction about writing in English. She immigrated to the United States in1983, and became a naturalized American citizen in 1993.She has taught, lectured and represented various colleges and universities including, Columbia University, University of Houston and Mount Holyoke College Amherst, Massachusetts. She held a prestigious Bunting Fellowship at Radcliff Harvard in 1986 and was visiting scholar at Rock Feller Foundation Center in Bellagio, Italy, 1991. She has been in advisory committee of former Pakistani Prime Minister, Benazir Bhutto. In 1991, she received Pakistan's highest national Award, *Sitara-e-Imtiaz* in the field of arts. She is also the recipient of National Endowment for Arts Grant in 1987. In 1991 she received a very prestigious A New York Times Book Review Award for her novel *Cracking India* (1989) originally published *as* The *Ice-Candy-Man* (1988). In1993 she got Lila Wallace-Reader's Digest Award worth 105,000 U.S.Dollars. She is one of those few women creative writers who depicted the undaunted resilience that women exhibited in the extreme chaotic times. In *Ice-Candy-Man* (1998), she represents number of women characters who fought and survived the most disastrous religious and political frenzy in the history of mankind. Despite their physical, emotional and economic weaknesses, her women characters asserted themselves amid patriarchal dominance. *Ice-Candy-Man* (1998) is in fact a realistic document of female suppression and marginalization. It presents a realistic picture how women are subjected and exploitation in patriarchal society. It exposes the untamed masculine power which is keen to assault women.

But what makes her noteworthy is her impartial delineation

of the partition of the Indian subcontinent and her religious distance from Hindus, Muslims and even Parsis. "She is best known for her collaborative work with Indo-Canadian film maker Deepa Mehta: Sidhwa wrote both the 1991 novel *Ice-Candy-Man* which served as the basis for Mehta's 1998 film *Earth* as well as the 2006 novel *Water.* A Novel based upon Mehta's 2005 film Water" (wikipedia.org/wiki/Bapsi_Sidhwa).

Deepa Mehta

Deepa Mehta is undoubtedly one of the finest women film-makers of Indian origin.

> What is unique about Deepa Mehta's filmography in Canadian cinema is not only her broad commercial success, but also her continued ability to bring her dual perspective to bear on both of her home countries, to continue making movies in India despite intense and sometimes violent protests. And to continue making movies in Canada despite ongoing funding battles. (Pike 266)

Born on 1st of January 1950 in Amritsar, she attended Welham Girls High School, a boarding school at Dehradun and graduated from Lady Sri Ram College for women, University of Delhi with a degree of Philosophy in 1973 and in the same year migrated to Canada. After completing her graduation she started making documentaries for television. She wrote scripts for children's film such as *Danger Bay,Inside Stories* and *the Young Indiana Jones Diary.* Initially she was drawn towards photography but later she shifted to the film making. She made an hour long television programme named *Travelling Light: the Photo journalism of Daleep Mehta,* which brought her much acclaim in the form of three Gemini nominations (Emmy Award Equivalent of Canada).*Sam and Me* (1991) was her first film. She has developed a well-earned reputation of innovative and courageous filmmaker whose movies often address the universal issue of identity and tradition.

She is one of the most provocative and exciting new directors to make the mark on world cinema at the turn of the millennium. She endeavours to explore the complex cultural taboos and tensions prevalent in Indian society through her films. Though she was more drawn towards photography than to film making. But cinema was in her blood. Mehta's father was a film distributor and owned a number of movie theatres, as a child Mehta watched hundreds of movies in her father's theatre but did not have an early interest in becoming a filmmaker. She grew in a film industry family. The family's fortunes rose and fell according to success of her father's latest releases. She grew up with cinema, with Friday night openings and Monday-morning grosses.

The year she started her career she met Paul Saltzman, a documentarian from Canada when he was in India making a film, married him and migrated to Canada. A daughter, Devyani Saltzman was born to her. While raising Devyani, she worked as script writer for children's film. In 1975 she made a documentary; *At 99: A Portrait of Lousie Tandy March*, depicting an almost centenarian who remained an active and vital Yoga practitioner.In 1983, Deepa and Paul divorced, a very painful moment, that forced Devyani to live with one of her parents when she was just eleven.She decided to live with father and consequently mother daughter relations were on tenterhooks for some years. In 1999, Mehta invited Devyani to Banaras to be the part of *Water* (2005) crew. After divorce, Mehta returned to film making with renewed zeal. Later she married to David Hamilton, who is also a film producer. On one occasion Devyani says that their relationships (mother-daughter) became lovable during shooting of *Water* and the invisible shirt of sadness had begun to melt. It was a huge moment for Deepa, who began sharing home with her daughter, much before she completed the film. The rebirth of *Water* coincided happily with the rebirth of her relationship with Devyani. Her first feature film as an individual director was *Sam & Me.* After this she made *Camilla* (1994). *Sam and Me*, won for her *Camera D' Or* award at 1991, Cannes Festival. It's a huge encouragement for her to go all out in film making career. In 1992, she directed another one hour episode of ABC-TV Series. *The Young Indiana Joes Chronicles* on location in Benares India.

In 1996, Mehta embarked on her elemental trilogy: *Fire, Earth* and *Water*. Commenting about Deepa Mehta and her elemental trilogy, Manju Jaidka writes: "Strong, controversial films like *Fire, Earth* and *Water* have made an impact and left indelible impressions on the viewers. Questioning prevalent social beliefs, they posit the other side of the truth that has been ignored so far" (77).

By now Mehta's stature as a director has grown internationally. Most of her films deal with women's issues. And all of her works are gender related. Talking about the reach and scope of her films Mehta, Manju Jaidka observes:

> Time and again, Mehta has been described as a transnational film-maker. This is another way of saying that although her films are about India, her concerns do not begin and end with India; they reach out to the world beyond, making connection, building bridges, exposing to the world facets of India that were not revealed earlier. (20)

She has very deep concern for Indian women who have been stifled from centuries by an oppressive social system. Her first film of elemental trilogy *Fire* which came in 1996 is about politics of sexuality. Originally the film was made in English which won fourteen international awards. Later, when it was dubbed in Hindi and was screened in India, it created nation-wide tumult. It is centered on the relationship between two unhappy unmarried

Indian women. The film has a lesbian content which is a taboo in India. And film and its director have to face the ire of Hindu fundamentalists. But the film was gladly accepted in the Western World. Second of the Mehta's elemental trilogy is *Earth* (1998) an adaptation of Bapsi Sidhwa's *Ice-Candy-Man*. Showering praise on Mehta, Wyndham Wise writes that Mehta has developed a well-earned reputation as innovative and courageous film maker whose movies often address the universal issue of identity and tradition. Declaring about her film making skills she herself says that she doesn't sit to write a script with ideas in mind, they seem to come out in her films.

This book gives thrust to explore and analyze how Mehta metamorphosed the Bapsi Sidhwa's much acclaimed novel *Ice-Candy-Man* into film *Earth*. The film *Earth* is a story about the partition of India. It is a film about women who became the victim of partition. This is a story of marginalization of women on both sides of the border. This film text brings the women to the center. Mehta's adaptation of film, told from the point of view of eight year old polio struck Parsi girl, Lenny was premiered at the 1998 Toronto Film Festival. After the release of this film Mehta started her another film *Water* (2005), which too raised a storm of anger from the Hindu Fundamentalists in the holy city of Varanasi. To make *Water* was a horrifying experience for Mehta. This film depicts the treatment widows receive at the hands of orthodoxy. This film exposes the priestly Hindu class which has been distorting religion for its own benefit. In this regard Manju Jaidka observes:

> *Water* draws our attention to certain prevalent codes of conduct that exist for both men and women; the difference is that codes for men are in their favour, upholding their right to lay down the rules in society. Interestingly, the codes for women are also in men's favour; it is almost like 'heads I

> win, tails you lose', the identity of women being determined primarily by her relationship with men-is she a wife or a widow? (8).

Hindu fanatics leveled death threats to Mehta. The set of *Water* was damaged and she was forced to shoot the film in Sri Lanka. Despite the threats and protests from all quarters, Mehta was rock solid in her determination to complete the film. Describing about her films, she says that she does not aim to be didactic. She does not uphold some personal ideology in her films. She makes films about the subject which interests her most. *Fire*, the first film of Elemental Trilogy series was adjudged the most popular Canadian film at Vancouver International Film Festival. It won several prestigious awards such as The Silver Rose for best Feature film at Verona's Love Screen Film Festival, The Audience Award at L.A and Fly Away Home, Canada People's Choice Award at Toronto International Film Festival. *Earth*, the second of the trilogy film is based on Sidhwa's critically acclaimed novel *Cracking India* which was first published *as Ice-Candy-Man*, was released in 1998. And finally *Water*, third of the elemental trilogy after a great deal of controversies was released in 2005. Transformation of novel into film and vice-versa within the feminist critique is the main focus of this book. All the selected texts are explored, analyzed and evaluated in the later chapters. The chapter wise essence of the book is as follow:

In Chapter I –'*Ice-Candy-Man* and *Earth* : A Hybrid Presentation of Literary and Visual Texts', a detailed analysis of Deepa Mehta's *Ice-Candy-Man* (1988) and its adaptation into a film *Earth* (1998) with its pros and cons in studied extensively. This chapter concentrates on the emergence, growth, process of transference, issue of borrowing from other sources, budget concerns, success and failure of the film version, fidelity concerns, commercial aspect and advantages and disadvantages associated with this conversion.

In Chapter II – 'Reading *Water* as Film and Novel', an attempt is made to study a literary phenomenon called novelization which is opposite to adaptation and deals with the transference of a film text into a literary text (film into novel). It answers question like what made Sidhwa write a novel based on a film. Why she picked up the film *Water*? Was it a judicious decision? Was she successful in conveying what she thought was unsaid in the film? This chapter deals with all these issues besides dwelling upon brief history of novelization. All merits and demerits linked with this type of conversion are critically analyzed and examined.

In Chapter III – 'Feminist Reading of Literary Texts – *Water, Earth* and Film Texts – *Earth, Water*', an argument is made to have an insight into the proposed texts: two film texts, *Earth* (1998) and *Water* (2005*) and* two literary texts (novels); *Ice-Candy-Man*(1988) and *Water*(2006) in feminist perspective.

Chapter IV – 'Film Texts – *Earth* and *Water* : Under the Lens of Feminist Film Theory', deals with the study of film texts under the scanner of feminist film theory. Both the films are studied in the purview of Feminist Film Theory. *Earth* and *Water* being the feminist film texts, Laura Mulvey's concept of 'Male Gaze' is taken into account to study both the film text. After going through an exhaustive and extensive study an attempt has been made to summarize the findings in the final Chapter – Conclusion.

Chapter-I

Ice-Candy-Man and *Earth*: A Hybrid Presentation of Literary and Visual Texts

A film is a movie cousin of a novel and both of these tell a story. However, they possess separate entities. Film adaptation has become a norm rather than an exception in literature. In fact, history of film is also the history of film adaptation. Birth and growth of film as an art has been deeply influenced by different literary genres especially by novels. The making of films, sourced from the literature gave rise to a never ending debate between the academicians and film makers because of inherent conceptual and perceptual differences. Custodians of literature stood against adaptation, which they thought it was for the coarse amusement of masses. Raymond Durgnat, a renowned British film critic opines that adaptation lacks the cultural prestige. In the beginning, the films almost solely depended on the novels for the source material. But there are critics who expressed their apprehensions about the narrativity and its fidelity to the source text. Film scholar Geoffrey Wagner, classified three modes of the film adaptation:

> *Transposition*, in which a novel is directly given on the screen with a minimum of apparent interference; the *commentary*, where an original story is taken and either purposely or

> inadvertently altered in some respect; and, the *analogy* (which) must represent a considerable departure for the sake of making another work of art. (64)

The screen writer's concern for fidelity and the audience's expectation for the film in relation to original work are taken into account. In this chapter the adaptation of *Ice-Candy-Man* into the film *Earth* is to be seen from screen writer's perspective and not as the replica of original source.

French Film Critic, Jean Mitry asserts that the adaptation of a novel into a film is based on the absurd assumption that there exist a content which can be transferred and transformed from one form of expression to another. The relation between film and novelis probably more than hundred years old. "A Film is a cinematographic representation of a story, drama, episode, event, etc. that is shaped, angled, finite, intended, whether it is a document or an art installation, a bit of gritty realism, or a full blown fantasy" (Michael Wood 114).But ever since the birth of films, film-makers had made films based on plays, short stories and novels ever since its birth. In fact, there is an endless list of novels which have been adapted into the films.There are shining examples of films that are inspired from the novels while there are others which have butchered the novels from where they have been adapted. As Araz Havana asserts:

> Both mediums have different elements that work in their favour that the other does not. A film has the visuals, audio and the human connection that a book could not physically create. Conversely, books have the invested time of the reader to expand on other details and give insight into characters that couldn't possibly be created in two hours of film. (dailycollegeon.com)

However, there is no dearth of people who disapprove of adaptation. Some view that it is impossible to adapt a novel into the rigour or rife with meaning into film, particularly a commercial film. But there are scholars who claim that the novel adapted into a film emerges as an artistic masterpiece. The debate in this regard is endless.

In this chapter a deep insight is made to explore and analyze the different aspects of adaptation with special focus on *Ice-Candy-Man* (1988) by Bapsi Sidhwa and its metamorphosis into a film the *Earth* (1998) by Deepa Mehta. An emphasis is made to examine the ideological implications of the given texts. In order to arrive at comprehensive understanding of the nature of adaptations, socio-cultural, politico-economic, psychological, feminist as well as technical implications are considered with special emphasis. The aim is to find out the answers of the following:

- What inspires Mehta to make a film based on a novel written by Sidhwa?
- What are the changes, if any, in the film?
- What are the inclusions and exclusions made in the film?
- Do these additions and deletions have any socio-cultural, psychological, gender-centered, historical, economic and technical overtones?
- Is there any difference in making political, social, cultural, economic statements between the original and adapted work?
- Who are the target audience of Sidhwa and Mehta?
- What are the economic implications of the novel and the film?
- Has the adapted work achieved the commercial success?
- Does the film adversely affect the novel from where it is adapted or it gives another life to the novel?

- Is there any difference in the characterizations and plot of *Ice-Candy-Man* and the *Earth*?
- How are women characters portrayed in the novel and the film?
- Beginning and ending of the novel and the film? The discussion proceeds with these questions in mind.

Of all literary genres, novels have been the popular choice of the film makers. Since the birth of film, literature has provided an extraordinary range of source material for film text. Best sellers have been metamorphosed into block-busters, the list is endless. Commenting on the influence of literature on the films, eminent film scholar Edwin McDowell writes in 'The York Times' (14 July 1985): "One in fifty novels published in this country were optioned by Hollywood" (1).

Similar comments are made by Hortense Powdermaker in his book Hollywood: *The Dream Factory* (1950). He points out that slightly less than forty percent films have been adapted from novels. But it is important to understand why film-makers adapt novels instead of creating their own stories? Which medium is more effective in eliciting a story? What is the need to transfer a novel or a literary text into a film? All these questions need answers.

Of all other mediums of expression, film in the present day world has become one of the most popular mediums. Today film and literature has become a serious academic pursuit. According to Louis D. Giannetti, "The overwhelming bulk of what's been written about the relationship of film and literature is open to serious question" (89).The relationships, resemblances and differences between the proposed texts need to be examined. The points where these merge and part company are explored and analyzed. A Film like any other art form has been adapted from the existing art. In the history of the arts, surely borrowing is the most frequently used mode of adaptation. Here the artist employs, more or less extensively the material, idea, or form of an earlier, generally successful, text. Adaptation is the transfer of a written work in a whole or in a part in to a feature film. In fact, it is the appropriation of creating meaning from the prior text and is a refraction of a particular artist's work in another artist's subconscious. Literature is a powerful tool in the hands of creative writers to present the world they see or they wish to be.

Making of the film *Earth*

In making *Earth,* Deepa Mehta sets herself a daunting task, equipped with cinematic tools and artistry in transforming Sidhwa's brilliant novel *Ice-Candy-Man* into a film. Sidhwa wrote a novel published *as Ice-Candy-Man* in India and England, but it was published as *Cracking India* by Sidhwa's American publishers Milkweed Edition in 1991 without any textual changes. It is a character-oriented title. It suggests a metonymic interpretation. Ice Candy Man is an important character in the novel and possesses several layers of connotative and enigmatic interpretations. It was feared that an American audience might take Ice Candy Man as a drug pusher. In an interview given to Raju Moza about the two titles of the novel, Sidhwa replies that the title of the book was renamed *Cracking India* in America since drug dealers are sometimes referred as "candy men" there.

However, in India it was published with the title *Ice-Candy-Man.* Ice Candy Man is a street vendor selling popsicles. The novel reveals the story of partition of the Indian sub-continent. But it took about a decade for the *Ice-Candy-Man* to be adapted into a movie the *Earth.* How did it happen? Revealing this fact Sidhwa tells interviewer Raju Moza:

Deepa Mehta came across the book in a store in Seattle and,

> attracted by title, read it. She had already made *Fire* and felt *Cracking India* would adapt well for the second film, *Earth*, in the trilogy. She called me from Canada to ask if she could base a film on the book and I promptly agreed. I think the movie accurately reflects the underlying theme of the chaos partition created in the Punjab. I think EARTH is a beautiful film...of course; a film is not a talking book.

That was how the idea of making film *Earth* occurred to Mehta.

Adaptation of Ice-Candy-Man(1988) into a Film Earth (1998)

Transformation of a novel (a literary text) to a film (visual text) is not just an extraction of dialogues from pages of books. Adapting a novel into a film is very elaborate, complex, ornate and high priced process. It involves a collaboration of several people such as director, script writer, cinematographer, musician, singers, set designers, distributers and most importantly the actors. Keeping all these in mind an utmost care is taken while making a film. A little lapse while transforming a novel into a film on the part of film-maker can destroy the entire project. Therefore what is to be added discarded and altered are very crucial issues taken into considerations. In order to establish an argument about comparing and contrasting the two different works of art, it is worthwhile to look into lives of both the artist.

Bapsi Sidhwa was born in Karachi and brought up in Lahore during pre-independent India. Though we cannot label her but undoubtedly she is as New York Times says, "Pakistan's finest English language novelist." She is Parsi Pakistani diasporic writer who stands on the fence to witness Hindu-Muslim-Sikh divide with double impartiality because Lenny being a child narrator in the novel *Ice-Candy-Man*. Being Parsi she does not belong to either of the communities that perpetrated havoc on each other. She seems likely to be more neutral and objective in giving the harrowing account of the partition. Talking about partition Col. Bharucha says,"I hope no Lahore Parsee will be stupid enough to court trouble, ...don't forget, we are to run with hounds and hunt with hare"(ICM 36-37). Only way to be out of trouble is to stay neutral. Telling the congregation of Parsis, Col. Bharucha further says, "As long as we do not interfere we have nothing to fear! As long as we respect the customs of our rulers-as we always have-we'll be all right! Ahura Mazda has looked after us thirteen hundred years he will look after us for another thirteen hundred!"(ICM 39). Directing the Parsis he further says, "As long as we conduct our lives quietly, as long as we present no threat to anybody, we will prosper right here" (ICM 40). Despite having these textual cues there is no doubt that *Ice-Candy-Man* presents a Pakistani perspective. Sidhwa herself admitted that this was a politically motivated novel.

> The political figures of the time, Mahatma Gandhi, Jawaharlal Nehru, Lord Mountbatten, Subhash Chandra Bose, and Mohammad Ali Jinnah are all named in the book and presented in an unfavorable manner. They are shown inconsistent, shifting from one position to another. In many books Gandhi is often extolled. But he is not spared in the *Ice-Candy-Man.* (Dhawan and Kapadia 21)

Talking about Gandhi, butcher in the novel says, "That non-violent, violence monger – your precious Gandhi – first he declares that Sikhs fanatics. Now suddenly he says: "Oh dear, the poor Sikhs cannot live with the Muslims if there is Pakistan!" What does he think we are – some kind of beast? Aren't they living with us now? 'He is a politician, *yaar,*' says Masseur Soothingly. "It's his business to suit his tongue to the moment" (ICM 91).

Deepa Mehta on the other hand was born into a Hindu family in Amritsar. She had her early education at Dehradun and had her graduation from Delhi University. She moved to Canada in 1973.Since them she had been shuttling between India and Canada. Though she is a transnational film maker yet her interests are deeply Indian especially about Indian woman. She represented travails of Indian woman on the screen and had a strong concern for them. *Fire, Earth* and *Water* are such films. *Earth* which has been adapted from the novel is about partition which caused mutual hatred, disharmony, divisiveness, suspicion, distrust; hostility among the communities which have been living in peace for centuries. Partition of India is the backdrop of the film *Earth* which has been adapted from the novel *Ice-Candy-Man*. Since the film *Earth* was largely meant for Indian audience, it was more inclined to represent Indian perspective. However, Both Sidhwa and Mehta delineated series of female characters who survived the chaotic time of 1947 when India was cracked into two nations. This event is registered as one of the worst communal, religious and political riots in the history of human kind. Both the artist tried to paint an impartial picture of the turmoil and the atrocities being inflicted on women during partition. Describing the event Manju Jaidka writes:

> The novel by Sidhwa focuses on the trauma of 1947 Partition of India. Narrated from a child's perspective, it transports its characters from the state of easy innocence to a horrendous epoch when terrifying atrocities are committed and the dismemberment of the Indian subcontinent takes place. (50)

Ice- Candy –Man is based on the tragedy which lurks closer to the world of Lenny, who lives in 1947 Lahore. She is introduced to the readers when she is just four years. Watching Ayah carry Lenny, an English gnome tut tuts: 'Let her walk. Shame! shame! Such a big girl in pram ! She's at least four!' (Sidhwa 2). She lives happily in the protected environment of a child, until political and social upheavals of the country completely shatter her world into bits and change the dynamics of her world. It is an account of the brutal world through the eyes of an innocent girl. Sidhwa, the author very astutely brought closer the different characters by having relationship with Lenny. She is very intimate with 18 years old, beautiful care taker Ayah. Sidhwa's novel *Ice-Candy-Man* depicts beautifully the inter-racial harmony of pre-Independence Lahore. And then we come across how people around Lenny change along racial, religious, regional, political and cultural lines and eventually do not hesitate to kill each other. Most trusted people betray the people they have trusted. Ice Candy Man betrays Lenny in extracting Ayah's hiding place. Lenny betrays Ayah mistakenly. The novel's climax is Ice Candy Man's betrayal of Ayah. It is an incredible novel which gives a moving account of a heart wrenching event in which twelve to fifteen million people were displaced from their homes and one to three million people were brutally massacred. It's a gripping tale that transports us to pre-India partition era. The book is a harrowing narrative of the physical, emotional anguish people suffered especially women. The representation becomes more compelling when presented through the point of view of Lenny from her personal perspective. She is pained to witness how in the times of turmoil, religion and gender both conspire to exploit women. She observes and describes everyday life including the things she was not supposed to know. The main arch of the story is that of Ayah, her nanny, who a Hindu woman is serving a Parsee family. During pre-partition many religious groups lived in mutual trust and peace. All seem to exist in harmony, Hindus, Muslims, Sikhs and even the Parses. All enjoy each other's company. Ayah is the center of attraction. Besides illuminating some facts about Sidhwa and Mehta, there is a need to draw attention towards the other facets of the two modes of expression employed by them.

Medium of Communication Language

The Language employed by Sidhwa in writing the novel is typically educated English of the British era interwoven with Punjabi. Sidhwa is very fluent in several languages such as English, Urdu, Guajarati and even Punjabi. But she opted to write in English. In an Interview to David Montenegro, she clarifies herself why she wrote in English. She tells him:

> I find myself comfortable writing in this language. My written Urdu is not very good, though I speak it fluently. As for Guajarati, hardly anyone in Pakistan knows the language. In Britain, of all places, people say, "Why don't you write in your own language?" And they bring very heavy political overtones to bear this. But I think, well, the English don't have monopoly on the language. It is the language of the world now. And it is a means of communication between various nationalities and the most immediate tool to hand. So I use it without any inhibitions or problems, so far I'm concerned. (Dhawan and Kapadia 12)

Besides, she was writing a novel meant for global readers. She chose to write in English but with frequent use of Urdu and Punjabi phrases. It gave the novel a local flavor and genuineness. She also uses Parsi proverbs in her other works. "Sidhwa feels that her writing style is influenced by her manner of speaking, which she calls a "salad of languages" (Dhawan and Kapadia 13). In her novel *Ice-Candy-Man*, this salad of language is mostly Punjabi and Hindi.

Teasing Lenny, roguish children clapping hands

chant,'*Langer deen! Paise teen! Tamba mota, pag mahin!*' Freely translated,'Lane Lenny! Three for a penny! Fluffy pants and fine fenny!" (ICM 3). Muccho shouting at her daughter yells,'Bitch! *Haramzadi!* May you die!'*Haram-khor! Slut, Work-shirker!* Some other words used in Hindi, Urdu and Punjabi are: *Phulka (miniature chappatis), arrey baba, paranthas, sarkar, granthi, swaraj, angrez, salaamalekum, mamajee, choorail, pakora, churidar, gulabjamun, jalebi, chichi, pahailwan, hullagoolla, janab, raj-karega-khalsa, akirahina koi, kirpan, sat sriakal! Bolay so nihaal!,'Allahaoakbar, yaaaaali, yaar, tamasha, paan, ladoo, baraat, ghoongat, sehra, doolha, chuddr, nimakharam.* She freely employed Punjabi and Urdu slangs and phrases and even sentences to give a real aroma of the then Lahore. As Dil Nawaz (*Ice-Candy-Man*) uses Urdu verses such as:

> *Kiya mujh ishk ne zalim ko aab ahista ahista*
> *Ke aatish gul ko karti hai gulab ahista ahista.*

Slowly, my love has compelled her, slowly-

The way the sun touches open the rose bud, slowly. (ICM 248)

Great Urdu poets like Iqbal, Ghalib, Zauq, Faiz too are translated by Sidhwa.Sidhwa's use of local languages imparts the narration a true flavour of the then-Lahore. The frequent use of Hindi, Urdu and some local phrases makes the novel authentic. English language by Sidhwa is to make the reach of the novel beyond the borders of India and Pakistan especially to western readers.Sidhwa is one of the finest writers of the sub-continent writing in English. She was not confined to Pakistan and India. She is a writer of global reach. And the best way to enlarge the scope of the novel beyond Pakistan and India was to write it in English. Keeping in mind the international readers, she wrote in English. But her choice to write in English was abandoned by

Mehta in her film *1947: Earth*. Mehta uses Hindi as medium of communication. Hindi is the language of masses. It is spoken in India and is understandable in Pakistan and even in Bangladesh. Unlike the novel, the film is a medium of masses. Novel is medium of literate and elite section of society, while a film is a mass medium catering to the needs of all. Mehta made the film in Hindi unlike that of her counterpart.

Use of Humor, Irony and Satire

Sidhwa is a wonderful novelist. She is very skillful in introducing humour, satire and irony even in the times of utmost difficulty. She makes the full use of these rhetorical devices in her novel *Ice-Candy-Man*. Conversation that goes on among the friends in Queen's Park is hilarious. Even during the most dark and hazardous times, Sidhwa's sense of humor is apparent in her novel. When Lenny is teased by street urchins, mother telling her the story of the little mouse with seven tails is simply amusing.

> Lenny's mother imitating mouse, sobs, "Mummy, Mummy, do something. The children at school tease me. They sing: 'Freaky mousy with seven tails! Lousy mousey with seven tails!" So the little mouse's mother chops off one tail. The next day the mouse again comes home complaining: Freaky mousey with six tails!" And so on, until one by one the little mouse's tails are all chopped off and the story winds to its inevitable and dismal end with baby mouse crying: "Mummy, Mummy, the children tease me." They sing, "Freaky mousey with no tail! Lousey mousey with no tail!" And there is no way the tail can be tacked back on. (ICM 6-7)

It is very amusing and helps in consoling the aggrieved Lenny. "Careful', says Masseur, whipping the bottle away. 'It'll grow hair on your fingertips.' 'Hey Ram!' says Ayah, quickly retracing her fingers, and rolling her eyes from one face to the next with fetching consternation" (p. 89 ICM).In Queens Park, Ice-Candy-Man, not to be out done in any type of conversation, talks about the first-class fertility pills The Government office Gardener was enthusiastic to try the pills. "Your wife's already produced children, hasn't she?" Tch! Not for her *yaar.* For myself. I feel old sometimes, 'confesses the graying gardener. 'It's not aphrodisiac. It's a fertility pill for women, 'explains Ice-Candy- Man. 'It's potent 'it can impregnate men!'(ICM 90).

However, Ice-Candy-Man's sense of humor appears to be impolite because it creates a startled silence. Sidhwa's expertise of storytelling is amazing. Humour and satire are an integral part of her world even if the dark clouds of danger loom large over the humanity. Sidhwa's expertise of storytelling is amazing. Humour and satire are an integral part of her world even if the dark clouds of danger loom large over the humanity.

But it's the genius of Sidhwa who very astutely instilled the sense of humor among her characters. "The imaginary fears of Lenny, Adi and their cousin are the source of humour but also a grim reminder of how rumour becomes institutionalized in highly surcharged atmosphere (Dhawan and Kapadia 43). Sidhwa's description of Ice Candy Man as a lunatic holy man is a rich source of humour. He appears in strange and striking attire. He enters Queen's Park. As Lenny Narrates:

> Thumping a five foot iron trident with bells tied near its base, the holy man lopes towards us, shouting: 'Ya Allah!'A Street, green, sleeveless, shift reaches to his hairy calves. His wrists and upper arms are covered with steel and bead bangles. And round his neck and chest is coiled a colossal hunk of copper wiring. He has become Allah's telephone! His holding the ends of copper wire in one hand and

> stretching the other skywards and then dialing the mystic numbers '786' and bringing an invisible receiver to his ear and starting conversation in Punjabi,"Allah ? Do you hear me, Allah? This poor woman wants a son! She has four daughters . . . one, two, three, and four! You call this justice?" (ICM 98)

His holding conversation with Allah is simply exhilarating. He pretends to talk to God on telephone 'Wah, Allah! 'Shouts Ice-Candy-Man. 'There is no limit to your munificence! To you king and beggar are same! To you this son-less woman is queen! Ah! The intoxication of your love! The depth of your compassion! The ocean of you generosity! Ah! Miracles of your cosmos! He shouts, working himself into state. (ICM 99) And bowing of *burka* clad woman in gratitude is very ludicrous. His antics provide a rich humour. Lenny finds his familiarity to God very alarming. 'He addresses God as 'tu' instead of using the more respectful 'tusi'. I'm sure I were the Almighty I'd be offended; no matter how mad the holy man!'(ICM 99). This is very amusing. Ice-Candy-Man's antics and utterances set Ayah rolling on the grass.

Deepa Mehta does not lag behind in presentation of humour in the film. The dinner party scene, in which the children hid themselves under the dinner table, is beautifully crafted. The visualization of the scene is superbly done. Aamir Khan as a holy lunatic has done a wonderful job as a through comedian. He leaves the audience with no option but to laugh boisterously. His strange attire is a rich source of visual humour.

Lenny's Growth and her Sexual Maturation

Lenny's growth and maturation is another important feature of Sidhwa's *Ice-Candy-Man.* This is in fact a very audacious attempt on the part of Sidhwa to describe the process of a girl's sexual maturation in the country like Pakistan. Commenting on this Subhash Chandra observes:

> It is a bold attempt on the part of a woman writer to take up the theme which is different from traditional issues the women writers generally assay-the issue of romantic involvements and the sentimental stuff. Also it is no mean achievement on Sidhwa's part to depict the process of sexual maturation of a young girl while living in the country like Pakistan where measure of freedom for women is considerably less than in India. (176)

Lenny observes her everyday life, including the things she is not supposed to know. She watches stub-handed beggars, holy men, hawkers, cart-drivers, coolies, cooks, cyclists and all sorts of men throwing covetous glances at Ayah. As Lenny herself divulges: "The covetous glances Ayah draws educate me. Up and down, they look at her. Stub-handed twisted beggars and dusty old beggars on crutches drop their poses and stare at her with hard, alert eyes. Holy men, masked in piety, shove aside their pretences to ogle her with lust (ICM 3). As she further narrates, "I keep an eye on Ice-Candy-Man's toes. Sometimes, in the course of an engrossing story, they travel so cautiously that both Ayah and I are taken unaware" (ICM 19). Lenny's relation with the cousin is also a step towards her sexual maturation. When he has returned from Quetta after he had hernia operation. 'Let me show you my scar,' he offers, unbuttoning his fly and exposing me to the glamorous spectacle of the stitched scar and a handful of genitals. He too has clever fingers. "You can touch it, he offers" (ICM 21). But Lenny does not allow him to manipulate her sexually. This is in fact a very courageous attempt on the part of Sidhwa to delineate a girl's sexual maturation. As Lenny herself says, "Though my faculties of reason, deduction and logic advance with the years" (ICM 21). Mehta too has portrayed Lenny in the same manner. But novel allows the writer more freedom and space as compared to the film maker.

Depiction of Vengeance Taken on Women's Body During the Time of Partition

Ice-Candy-Man is the novel that attracts interests on several accounts. It is a novel dealing with the theme of partition. Sidhwa depicts the events of partition in their naked cruelty. It depicts the callousness that was inflicted by males on the females during the times of partition. The stories of defeats and triumphs were celebrated with vengeance on a women's body. *Ice-Candy-Man* is novel that manifests female discourse unlike that of Khushwant Singh's *Train to Pakistan* (1956). But the novel *Ice-Candy-Man* has many women characters who come across oppression and exploitation. This was the time when thousands of women were kidnapped and killed. Thousands left alive only to be raped again and again. *Ice-Candy-Man* is about the wounds that are inflicted especially upon women. Sidhwa had managed to evoke the great political upheavals of the age through a young girl's mind. She has done a commendable job in bringing the deep rooted religious, political, social, cultural and economic tensions to the surface. Her juxtaposition of innocence and experience through Lenny's observation is brilliant. *Ice-Candy-Man* as a novel presents the history of partition in a miniature scale. But it reveals this event more vividly than mere statistics about the number of people uprooted from their homes, kidnapped, killed and raped. The novel deals with life the people led and the real implications of partition. The partition of India was the greatest defining moment in the history of the country. Withdrawal of British regime was not a simple event, it brought with it uncontrolled chaos replete with unlimited atrocities. Describing the magnitude of the calamity partition brought with it, Manju Jaidka writes:

> History books give us the details-the grim, dry statistics, how many million people were uprooted, how many killed, the number of women who suffered in various ways, the loss of property, and so on. The litany is endless. This is the story of the partition that has come down to us from the older generation which lived through the trauma, survivors whose scars never to heal fully. (48-49)

Khushwant Singh's *Train to Pakistan* (1956), Bhisham Sahni's *Tamas* (1974) and Manto's *Toba Tek Singh or Cold Meat* (1955) are other works which depict this horrendous political event with socio-cultural and politico-economic impacts. Stating about the calamity, the partition brought with it, Urvashi Butalia writes: 'The predominant concerns of partition literature are often cited rupture, protest and repair (7). Sidhwa successfully depicted all these elements.

The Indian government estimated that about 83000 women were abused, abducted and raped during partition. Out of this number 50000 were Muslim women and 33000, Non-Muslim women. Meera Patel in her blog mentions that historical consensus supports a figure of 12 million people displaced, although the BBC suggests figure as high as 14.5 million people. This was a sort of undeclared civil war between Hindus-Sikhs and Muslims.

Ayah is portrayed as the worst victim of the partition in both the novel as well as in the film. She is abducted by the mob led by the man who once loved her. She was ravished and raped by the hoodlums. She is the victim of male aggression. She was kept as mistress for few months by the Ice candy man. She was forced to marry him and then kept in the *kotha*. She was pushed into prostitution. All types of atrocities were inflicted on her.

Deepa Mehta's film depicted Ayah as the final victim of the

partition. But the fright of partition is somewhat eased in the film by giving an emphasis on the romantic element. Ayah-Hassan relationship is wonderfully portrayed in the film. This attempt on the part of Mehta is certainly praise worthy. The inclusion of romantic element in the film eases the prevalent tension. Here Mehta seems to score points for the film as it is adapted from the novel.

Sidhwa and Mehta's Perspective of Partition

Sidhwa in her novel *Ice-Candy-Man* subtly depicts the three aspects of the partition: the ripping apart of India, the brutality ensued with ruthless carnage of the people, and the curing process. During partition, Sidhwa's little cosmos consisting of Hindus, Muslims, Sikhs, and Parsi have only one unifying entity – Ayah. She is presented as a unifying agent during the times of pre-independence India. But in the later part she becomes the victim of political acrimony. As the argument is flared up between all the friends at Queen's park, Ayah stands up smoothing the pleats in her limp cotton sari,"If you all talk of nothing butthis Hindu-Muslim business, I'll stop coming to the park," she says pertly (ICM 92). As Sidhwa describes it as "Only the group around Ayah remains unchanged. Hindu, Muslim, Sikh, Parsi are, as always, unified around her" (ICM 197). The fear lurks in every heart as the rumours about partition began to spread. As Sidhwa puts it in Lenny's mouth:

> There is much disturbing talk. India is going to be broken. Can one break a country? And what happens if they break it where our house is? Or crack it further up on Warris Road? How will I get to Godmother's then? It is perturbing that the people who are friends and have been living in love and fun irrespective of the faith and religion today become aware

> of their religious differences next day. Sidhwa describes it through Lenny as, "It is sudden. One day everybody is themselves-and the next day they are Hindu, Muslim, Sikh, Christian. People shrink dwindling into symbols. Ayah is no longer just my all en-compassing Ayah-she is also a token. (ICM 93)

Sidhwa's second aspect of partition is the violence that was perpetrated on women. Women irrespective of religion, caste, creed and sect were the victims. The women belonging to Hindus, Muslim and Sikhs were terrorized, kidnapped, raped and killed. Describing Ayah's abduction, Sidhwa writes:

> They drag Ayah out. They drag her by arms stretched taut, and her bare feet – that want to move backwards – are forced forward instead. Her lips are drawn away from her teeth, and the resisting curve of her throat opens her mouth like the dead child's scream less mouth...The men drag her in grotesque strides to the cart and their harsh hands, supporting her with careless intimacy, lift her into it. Four men stand pressed against her, propping her body upright, their lips stretched in triumphant grimaces. (ICM 183)

But the third aspect of Sidhwa's partition is that of a process of recovery. Not to be out done, all the women characters in the novel exhibit an extraordinary resilience. Sidhwa seems to score points over Mehta in this connection because film does not depict the process of recovery. She depicts the first two aspects quite beautifully. But the third aspect is lacking in the film because the film ends with the abduction of Ayah. Mehta does not want to restart the film after it has attained catastrophe. In this regard Mehta is herself of the opinion that there is no point to restart the film after catastrophe. She opines that for her the film ends with

Ayah's abduction. Quoting an interview with Deepa Mehta, Manju Jaidka writes: " In the same way, when she is asked about the portions of the novel by Bapsi Sidhwa that she does not include in her film, *Earth,* she shrugs indifferently to show her lack of interest in the subject:"For me, the FILM was dramatically over after ayah gets kidnapped" (82).

Is Ice-Candy-Man as an Impartial Partition Document?

Ice-Candy-Man is an impartial representation of partition. It is written in 277 pages and traces the history of events leading to partition and also gives an account of Lahore preceding the partition. Being Parsi, she portrayed her characters impartially without any favour or disfavour, sitting on a fence. In an interview to Gutman, Sidhwa explains that there was a struggle between the Hindus and Muslims, and as a Parsee she could give a dispassionate account of this huge momentous struggle.

Nevertheless to regard this novel as completely impartial is unfair. She seems to give a slight edge to the Pakistani perspective. Politically she appears to have her deepest sympathy for Pakistan. But on the other hand the film version of the novel is more inclined to represent Hindu perspective. Since the film was made for Indian audience, it favoured Indian point of view. But broadly the film too is an impartial representation as it is hued more in romantic colour. An extensive argument is made at this juncture with respect to the consequences of the transformation *of Ice-Candy-Man* into the film *Earth.*

The film *Earth* based on the novel *Ice-Candy-Man* came a decade later. Initially Sidhwa was somewhat dubious about the film version of the novel. But Mehta was sure about her film. She even refutes some of the suggestions given by Sidhwa. While watching a scene, Sidhwa wanted to give suggestion to Mehta.

The scene is "When raffish Ice Candy Man (Aamir Khan) hands over a cashe of stolen coins to the Ayah (Nandita Dass), Sidhwa feels he should not close her hands. Let her palm be open, as in the book, when she tells him she won't have the gold. Mehta hears of Sidhwa's suggestion and says, "Please don't even do this again? There is only one director on the set." Mehta was very sure about her plot, characters and actions. When the film was completed, Sidhwa loved it and says that it took some time to realize that Deepa could not have all the characters she had in her book. Appreciating Deepa she tells India Today that she has given her baby (Book) to Mehta in full trust. And Mehta has made an honest, beautiful, splendid and touching film.

In India the film was released as titled*1947: Earth.* With the release of the film, the book which had already been a critical success got wider recognition. It was Mehta's second film of her Elements trilogy. First being *Fire* and the third was *Water*. It is a film depicting the tragedy of partition through the eyes of a group of friends who live in Lahore, then the part of India. The film visualizes and recreates history of Hindus, Muslims, Sikhs, Parsees and even some Christians during the time of partition. How the people who have been living in harmony are at daggers drawn during this extraordinary historical event that shook the Indian Sub-continent to its very roots. The film is told as a melodrama and romance. Sidhwa's *Ice-Candy-Man*, from where this film has been adapted won her a top literary award in Pakistan, while the film was banned there. The film experienced many cuts from censor. Even the gentle and sweet sex scene and five other scenes were censored. And at the box office film proved a flop. The story of the film is set in the time before the partition of 1947. It is directed by Mehta and is produced by Anne Mason and Mehta herself. Cinematographed by Giles Nuttgens, music is given by A.R. Rehman and is edited by Barry Ferrel. It has a running length of 101 minutes and has a star cast of Aamir Khan (Dil Navaz or the Ice Candy Man),Nandita Das (Shanta or Ayah), Rahul Khanna (Hassan, the Masseur), Maia Sethna (Lenny Sethna), ShabanaAzmi (the female voice-over, older Lenny), Kittu Gidwani (Bunty Sethna), Kulbhushan Kharbanda (Imam Din), Arif Zakaria (Rustom Sethna), Rajender Kumar (Refugee Police), Pawan Malhotra (Butcher). Divulging about the film, Richard Phillips states that the *Earth,* by Deepa Mehta is an intelligent and deeply moving personal account of the partition. She depicts the partition of August 1947 when departing British Colonial rulers announced the division of the subcontinent into a Muslim-controlled Pakistan and a Hindu-Sikh dominated India. Without much deliberation about the consequences of partition, the Britishers pushed India into one of the worst human made tragedies. About 11 million people-Muslims, Hindus, Sikhs, Parses and many others found themselves in the wrong sides of the dividing lines. Deepa Mehta portrayed this human tragedy in a miniature scale in the film *Earth* through the eyes of Lenny, an 8 years-old, crippled Parsee girl. All live in harmony until British decided to quit India but not before dividing it in two nations on the basis of religious faith.

The film quickly comes to the main issue of partition. Hiding under the dinner table Lenny and her cousin came to know about the bitter quarrel between Singh and British Inspector of Police. Every day jokes play and mirthful activities at the Queen's Park are replaced by hostility, malice, bickering and callous remarks over the each other's religion. In the film, the leaders of the religious, political and ethnic groups begin lobbying for positions with British Authorities, leaving behind the masses especially women and children to be kidnapped, raped and killed. *Earth*, the film depicts the romance during times of anarchy and political and religious mayhem. Ayah-Hassan love alleviates the prevailing tension because of ensuing partition.

The film depicts the element of romance during the times of political anarchy and religious turmoil. Hassan seems to urge his friends to stay together and not to be swept away by their religious feelings. Ayah-Hassan, love blossoms even in this pandemonium. *Ice-Candy-Man* (Aamir Khan), another Muslim youth vying for Ayah's affection, happens to see Ayah-Hassan making love. Besides, the reports of the brutal killings, the train coming from Gurdaspur loaded with dead bodies and gunny sacks full of chopped off women's breasts, becomes pitiless even to the woman he loves. Such is the disgust, love and religion could provoke. There are all around tensions inflamed by all sorts of reports of murder, kidnaps, mass suicides, rapes and killings. *Ice-Candy-Man* outraged by jealousy and overwrought by mob atmosphere, leads a group of Muslim rioters to Lenny's house, demanding the removal of all Hindu servants, including the woman he loved (Ayah). All attempted to protect Ayah, claiming that she has left to Amritsar. Lenny, trusting *Ice-Candy-Man* admits that Ayah is still in the house. Ayah is dragged by the rioters, led by the man who loves her. Lenny's innocent mistake haunts her for the rest of her life. *Earth*'s in fact a very courageous and humane film by Deepa Mehta. Stating about the film Stephen Holding says that Earth is, "a powerful and disturbing reminder of how a civilization can suddenly crack under certain pressures" (6).

The film *Earth* by Mehta, screened one of the most terrible events of the 20th century. *The characters in the film denounced partition. Film's protagonists listening to a radio broadcast by Congress Party leader Jawaharlal Nehru declaring: "At the stroke of the midnight hour [August 15, 1947], when the world sleeps, India will awake to life and freedom."* Ironically, these comments are welcomed with distrust and doubt. One of the characters later declares that independence from the British will be drenched in our brother's blood. The cast of the film has done a very commendable job. Maia Sethna in Lenny's role, Nandita Dass as Ayah, Aamir as *Ice-Candy-Man,* Rahul Khana as Hassan and all characters have done justice to their roles in depicting this humane drama. Eulogizing Aamir Khan, Suparn Verma notes that Aamir Khan has probably given the best performance of his life. It is hard to imagine another actor bringing alive the nuances of the *Ice-candy-man* the way he does.

Music and Song in the Film Earth

A.R. Rehman's music with lyrics by Javed Akhtar combines to make *Earth*, a potent work of art. The film exposes the religious, political, regional and economic prejudices to the surface. It was in fact a very honest attempt by Mehta. Despite having proved a flop at box office, Aniket Joshi in Planet Bollywood gave film a 9.5 out of 10 and stated that, the *Earth* is strongly recommended to those who want to see a different type of Hindi film and who are tired of the usual boy meets girl stories and revenge dramas. There are films made by Mehta which saw good commercial success. To achieve a good commercial success is not an aim of Mehta. In this regard, David L. Pike writes:

> What is unique about [Deepa] Mehta's filmography in Canadian Cinema is not only her broad commercial success, but also her continued ability to bring her dual perspective to bear on both of her home country, to continue making movies in India despite intense and sometimes violent protests, and to continue making movies in Canada despite ongoing funding battles. (266)

In the Asian Film Festival, *Earth* (1998) bagged the Best Film Award. Rahul Khanna, who started his career with this film, got

'Best Male Debut Award'. The film made official entry for the 1999, 72nd Academy Award for Best Foreign Film, but could not make its way to the final five nominees selected by AMPAS. Roger Ebert states that Earth, "is effective because it doesn't require much history from its viewers, explains what it needs to be known, and has universal message" (rogerbert.com/review/Earth1999).

Ice-Candy-Man and Earth: Additions and Omissions

Mehta's adaptation of *Ice-Candy-Man* into the film *Earth* has many interesting additions as well as omissions. Novel and film are two different mediums, each having some advantage or disadvantage over the other. Characters in the novel come to us through language whereas characters in the film come to us through visual images. Commenting about this film, commentator, Michael Orme states, "We cannot transpose any one character from page to screen and hope to present him entirely as the novelist created him or the novelist's public knew him...who can really recall, having seen a screen performance which really and truly portrayed his favourite character as he knew it" (368).

In her selection, Mehta excludes certain female characters such as Slave sister, Godmother, Electric Aunt and Hamida. The film adaptation tends to sacrifice "extra" characters from the novel. It also ignores some important conversation of the novel. Lenny is the narrator and hence, interpreter of everything in the novel, but the film does not accord her the status. Many instances like Lenny's frequent visits to the house of Godmother, her conversation with Gandhiji, the mother's use of petrol to help move women across the border are completely absent in the film *Earth*. A whole section called "Ranna's story" which describes the bodily suffering of a Muslim boy and occupies substantial importance in the novel, is reduced to an insignificant short narrative by a nameless boy at the camp in the film. Mehta excludes some other characters, but retains some of their scenes and assigns those to other characters, i.e. Masseur gives Ayah a ride in his cycle in place of Sharbat Khan, Ice-candy-man threatens to drop Lenny suspended from the air instead of her brother Adi. Mehta's adaptation of *Ice-Candy-Man* into *Earth* is a serious artistic venture.

Use of Literary Tools in the Novel and Cinematic Tools in the Film

Both the '*Ice-Candy-Man* 'and the film '*Earth* 'use different tools to express the same idea. The novel uses tools such as symbol, simile, metaphor, allusion, paradox, irony whereas film uses various cinematic tools such as frame, shot, freeze, fades, color, light, sound, songs, voice-overs etc. As the novel *Ice-Candy-Man* is adapted into the film *Earth* certain changes are inevitable as there is a shift in the medium. As Manju Jaidka states:

> With Mehta's adaptation the narrative undergoes a generic transformation-from written words contained within the covers of a printed text it becomes an audio-visual presentation on the silver screen, portraying a historical event in the popular Bollywood style, with some songs and dance. (47)

Both Sidhwa and Mehta used very effectively the different tools in their novel and films respectively.

Use of Voice-over in the Film

Miriam Webster Online Dictionary defines voice-over as a production technique where a voice – that is not a part of narrative (non-diegetic) is used in radio, television production, film making, theatre or other productions. It is read from a script and may be spoken by someone who appears elsewhere in the production by some specialist voice actor. Mehta uses a female voice-over of Shabana Azmi for Lenny, the narrator in the novel *Ice-Candy-Man* (1998). As the cast is introduced, first the word *Earth* appears on the screen followed by 1947. Lenny is sitting in the chair with the map of India in front of her and is found scribbling with crayons on the map. The female voice-over of Shabana Azmi sounds:

> I was eight years old, living in Lahore in March 1947 when British Empire in India started to collapse. Along with talks of India's Independence from British came rumbling about its division into two countries, Pakistan and India. Hindus, Muslims, and Sikhs who had lived together as one entity for centuries suddenly started to clamour for pieces of India for themselves. The arbitrary line of division to British control to carve up India in August 1947 would scar the sub-continent forever. (Earth)

With this voice-over the film starts, and straightway we came across the rumours about partition. The shift from a young Lenny narrating the novel to an adult voice-over as the narrator in the film indicates from the beginning the kinds of changes that would take place in Mehta's film. Another voice-over of Shabana Azmi as an old Lenny plays at the end of the film after Ayah's adduction. It sounds:

> Two hundred and fifty years of British Empire ended in 1947. But what is there to show except for a country divided. The massacres and kidnapping vendettas and more violence, was it all worth? Fifty years have gone by since I betrayed my Ayah, Some say she married to Ice-Candy-Man, some say they saw her in a brothel in Lahore, others say they saw her

> in Amritsar. But I never set eyes on her again. And that day in 1947, when I lost Ayah, I lost large part of myself. (Mehta)

These are the last lines of the film coming from the voice-over of Shabana Azmi (older Lenny). It cannot be denied that certain omissions become essential to translate a novel to the screen due to the difference between written and visually auditory media. While Sidhwa's novel comprises of 277 pages, the screenplay for the film had to be shortened to fit the 101 minutes feature film length.

Earth the Film as a Slice of the Novel *Ice-Candy-Man*

The film *Earth* is a smaller version of the text from where it is inspired. We see a kind of condensation of the characters in the film. The novel represents the Lahore of 40s and 50s in detail. We can relive the then Lahore in the pages of *Ice-Candy-Man* whereas the film does not delve into it because of its time as well as other limitations. Sidhwa reveals the time of pre-partition, partition and post-partition while Mehta focuses more on the partition aspect. Sidhwa describes the events and characters through words while Mehta uses moving images in her portrayal of the characters and incidences. She uses images hued in emotions. In this regard, Manju Jaidka states:

> Taking a look at the written text, we note that the book comprising 277 pages not only traces the history of the events leading to the cracking of the Indian Sub-continent, but also gives us a graphic account of Lahore during the years preceding the partition and a sketch of the Parsi community during the times-its history and background, its ability to merge with the environment, and its neutral position in the political turmoil. (51-52)

The film *Earth* omits the first 60 pages of the novel and straightway leads to the ensuing danger of partition at the dinner party. The party is held in Mr. Singh's House, attended by Mr. Rogers, his wife Mrs. Rogers, Mr. Singh and his American wife along with the host. The film also skips the last 90 pages of the book. Chunks of the novel are excluded from the film. Despite squeezing 277 pages novel into a film of 101 minutes, Mehta had been very faithful in representing the historical events that figure the setting of the story – the partition. The novel focuses on the trauma of cracking India from child's perspective. Lenny is established as a firm witness to the riots, kidnaps, killings and rapes that marred and charred the city of Lahore. Though the film *Earth* focuses on the Ayah-Lenny, Ayah-Masseur, and Ayah-Ice Candy Man relations. Ayah is a common center, symbolizing undivided India. She is like magnet to all, irrespective of age, colour and religion. The film comes to an end depicting Ayah being dragged by fanatically crazy mob; being led by the man who loves her while the novel devotes 90 pages after this brutal incident.

Song-Music-Dance: a Motif of the Film *Earth*

Right from the dawn of Indian cinema, inclusion of songs is indispensable. The first sound film *Alam Ara* (1931) by Ardeshir Irani has seven songs. In the same year film *Shirheen Frahad*(1931) by Jamshedji Framji Madan, had as many as 42 song sequences. However, six to ten songs were usually featured in each film. Despite being an integral part of films, the eminent film-maker Satyaji Ray discarded the song and dance motif. The songs are composed and crafted with lyrics by eminent poets, set to music by musicians, and brilliantly choreographed to match the script of the film. Sung by professional playback singers and lip-synched by the actors. Interestingly, the songs appear to be sung by the characters themselves rather than being played in the background.

Sound and music play a very vital role in the visual medium especially in films. Sound imparts liveliness to the visual image. Sangita Gopal while expressing her views about the inevitability of the Hindi songs writes that Bollywood songs, along with dance, are a characteristic motif of Hindi cinema which gives it enduring appeal and a cultural value.

Keeping in mind the popular taste of the audience of Indian subcontinent, Mehta introduced songs in the film *Earth.* First song: *Ruth Aa Gayee Re, Ruth Chaa Gayee Re. Peeli Peeli Sarson phule, Peele Peele Patte Jhoomain. Peehu Pehuu Papiyah Bole. Chal Baag Main*....This song is cinematographed on advent of the spring and depicts the happy and festive atmosphere before an impending doom. The song is beautifully crafted by Mehta.The cutting of kite string shown in this song sequence by *Ice-Candy-Man* reveals his temperament. This song is sung by Sukhwinder Singh, composed by Javed Akhtar and music is given by A.R. Rehman. Second song: *Bano Rani Tumhe Sayaani, Hona hi tha, Hona hi tha. Ek Raja ki tumko Rani Hona Hi Tha, Hona Hi Tha..Banne Raja Key Ghar. Doli Mai JaKar.Hum Sakhiyon se Yun. Anjaan Hona hi Tha Hona hi Tha*...The lyrics of this song are written by Javed Akhtar, music given by A.R. Rehman and is sung by Sadhna Sargam. This is a marriage song sung on the occasion of Papoo's marriage. She is child bride and is given off in marriage to an old man. All the admirers of Ayah assemble on this occasion. And Ice-Candy-Man takes an opportunity to dance with Ayah (Shanta). The third song in the film is sung by renowned singer Asha Bhosle, composed by Javed Akhtar and the music is given by A.R.Rehman. The song: *Ye jo zindagi hai koi dastaan hai, Kab ho ga kya yeh khabar kahan hai,Yeh jo zindagi hai koi karvaan hai,Kahan jayegi ye khabar kahan hai-2. Jo afssane dil ney buney, Unko koi dil hi suney, Hum hauley hauley pyaar ki dhundhli fizayon mein aaye, Gehre gehre hai khwaab ki neeli ghatoyon key ssaye,*

Hum tum dono khoye khoye. This song is sung by Sriniwas, lyrics by Javed Akhtar, music by A.R. Rahman. The song depicts Ayah-Hasan love achieving physical bliss. Ice-candy-man watches Ayah-Hassan making love and is filled with nothing but hatred for both. He felt betrayed. Already smoldering Ice-Candy-Man becomes volcano to erupt any moment. The brutal murder of Hassan in a Muslim dominated area seems to have no mystery but *Ice-Candy-Man's* hatred for him. His betrayal of innocent Lenny to find Ayah seems to be the culmination of Hasan's murder. The film reveals that under the garb of prevailing political and religious hatred, the personal scores are also settled. This song symbolizes the impending danger and the uncertainty of life.

Another song in the film *Earth*: *Raat ki Daldal hai gaadhi re gaadhi re, Dhadkan ki chale kaise gaadhi re gaadhi re*-Lyrics by Javed Akhtar, sung by Sukhwinder Singh and music given by A.R. Rehman. This song describes the impending danger looming large in all directions. It signifies darkness, pessimism, terror and desperation. And the last song: *Ishwar allah tere jahanmein, Nafrat kyun hai jung hai kyun, Tera dil to itna bada hai,Insaan ka dil tang hai kyun*- This song is sung by Anuradha Sriram and Sujata Mohan, composed by Javed Akhtar and music given by A.R. Rahman. Not only songs but dance too is an integral part of Hindi film. The Indian audience is obsessed with songs and dances in the film. They cannot imagine a film without these two elements in the film. The music-song-dance aspect imparts not only color to the film but helps in pushing the story move forward. As Gokul Singh states, "Hindi film songs are now embedded in North India's popular culture and routinely encountered in North India in marketplaces, shops, during bus and train journeys and numerous other situations" (130).

The introduction of song and dance element in the film *Earth* makes it a source of pleasure and entertainment. In this regard,

Manju Jaidka observes: "With Mehta's adaptation the narrative undergoes a generic transformation-from written words contained within the covers of a printed text it becomes an audio-visual presentation on the silver screen, portraying a historical event in popular Bollywood style, with song and dance" (47).

Absence of Healing and Recovery Process in the Film *Earth*

The film *Earth* focuses on the two aspects; The Cracking of India and the violence that followed. The third aspect which gives emphasis on the healing process is absent in the film while the novel brings to light the resilience of the women and their fight to resist male dominance. All the women characters like Ayah, Mother, Godmother, Mucho, Slave Sister, Lenny and Hamida represent a way of life that in one way or the other challenges the patriarchal repressiveness. They display extraordinary resilience and undaunted spirit during nerve shattering episode of partition. Godmother plays a very vital role in the novel after Ayah's abduction. She becomes the force to reckon with. As Lenny states, "No baby-not even a kitten-is delivered within the sphere of her influence without her becoming instantly aware of its existence" (ICM 210). She emerges as the most influential character after Ayah's kidnapping. Godmother reprimands *Ice-Candy-Man* when he came to her, explaining his faithfulness to Ayah. His stream of brash talk fails to make on impact on Godmother. Her stony silence overpowers his poetic outburst. When he recites Faiz:

> *"Tum aye ho na shab-e-intezar guzri hai-.*
> *Talash main hai seher baar baar guzri hai!*(ICM 245)

'Shabash! Well said!' says Godmother..."You have been a gifted poet! And not, as rumored, a Mandi pimp!" (ICM 245-246). She takes on him to defend Ayah. She is not convinced by his oily tongue when he says that Ayah is to him an angel and a goddess and he is a slave to her. He worships her and says that she can come to no harm with him. To this Godmother reacted like scorpion ready to strike and says:

> You permit her to be raped by butchers, drunks, and *goondas* and say she has come to no harm".... 'Is that why you had her lifted off – let hundreds of eyes probe her-so that you could marry her? You would have your own mother carried off if it suited you! You are shameless badmash! *Nimakharam* Faithless. (ICM 248)

No amount of threats, pleading, remonstrance, bellows, declamations, courtly manners, resourcefulness or wailing could impede Ayah's registration to Recovered Women's Camp on WarrisRoad. Finally, weak, neglected and moon struck *Ice-Candy-Man,* stations patiently at Phailbus's wall as Ayah is taken by a Sikh guard to Mr. Phailbus for homeopathic treatment. Lenny, the narrator in the novels says,"Often I accompany Ayah to Mr.Phailbus's; and when we past the Ice-candy- man, he greets us courteously and does not stare at Ayah, but casts his eyes down. Ayah behaves as if he is invisible" (ICM 277). When he recites Ghalib's couplet revealing his plight. Ayah behaves as if he is inaudible too. She is unresponsive and indifferent to the man who has betrayed her. The beautiful lines of Zauq, Iqbal, Ghalib fail to make a slightest impact on Ayah.

Sidhwa's narrative speaks of this process of recovery but Mehta's film does not. *Earth* the film, omits the last 90 pages of the novel, the portion that followed the abduction of Ayah (Shanta), bringing in the recovery and rehabilitation of hapless women. By concluding the story of Shanta where she does, Deepa Mehta underscores the futility of all so called 'recovery' or healing operations. She says that once the sanctity of a woman has been defiled, so to speak, can there be any going back? Can one make amends? Can the clock be turned back? Is any form of redress or compensation enough for the loss suffered by woman? In other words, after such a transgression, what forgiveness? But contrary to film, the novel deals with recovery and rehabilitation of the victims, certainly a very soothing experience for the reader.

Ayah : An Epitome of Resilience

Ayah is not to be melted by Ice-candy-man's feigned or genuine concern for her. But she (Shanta) becomes an easy target, a scapegoat, a symbol of the 'other'. As Jaidka asserts, "The Ayah is exposed to violence because of her radiant sexuality, her bouncy walk and rotund appeal. Devoid of these attractions she would be as unappealing as the narrator's Godmother, perhaps who binds her breasts and has no sex appeal" (54). All women including Ayah, Godmother and Lenny saw *Ice-Candy-Man* as treacherous, dangerous, and contemptible and a destructive force that must be wiped out. Godmother dismisses him saying, "Get out of my sight, you whining haramzada!...You have trapped her in poisonous atmosphere of the *kotha*" (ICM 249-250). When he tries to convince Godmother that he has married her, she rebukes her by saying, "There is no God for the likes of you *shaitan*!" (ICM 250). She further asks him: 'When did the marriage take place?' He replies, 'In May'. She relentlessly rebukes him thundering: "She was lifted in February and you married her in May? What were you doing all the time? Why don't you speak? Can't you bring yourself to say you played the drums when she danced? Counted money while drunks, peddlers, sahibs, and cut-throats used her like a sewer?"(ICM 250). Godmother is in no mood forgive him for the villainy he committed. Such is the power Godmother displayed to guard Ayah from any venomous fang that could strike her. She very emphatically says that she has nothing to be ashamed of. The strangers who lifted her in the carts have shamed her. The men she counted among her friends and admirers such as Imam Din, Sharwat Khan, Butcher and Ice candy man, they have ashamed her. Ayah too displayed a tremendous courage to go to Amritsar. She is not in mood to forgive the monster who has killed her spirit and mutilated her 'angel's voice'.

Screening of Novel into a Film: A Mammoth Task

Screening a novel into a film is not a mean task. It requires a tremendous talent for a director to turn words into moving images. Dore Schary, a noted writer and film producer is right when he argues that the screen writer's task is to sit down and word by word create images. As the novel *Ice-Candy-Man* undergoes transformation into a film *Earth,* there is shift in narratology. As Imelda writes:

> After all, the process of presenting a literary text on film is one in which the stock formal devices of narrative – point of view, focalization, tense, voice, metaphor-must be realized by quite other means, and this is where the creative mettle of the adapter is put supremely to the test. (9)

Mehta has been highly successful in using the filmic narrative devices in her all her films especially *Fire, Earth* and *Water.*

Eye versus Camera

Camera plays a vital role in presenting the point of view in the film. It shows what it sees without any favour or bias. Both the novel and the film are different mediums of expression. As there is shift in medium the narrative also changes. Bluestone notes that "the novel has three tenses the film has only one" (48). The camera never discriminates as Imelda puts it like this: "In the case of point of view, we move to from narrative focalization to *mise-en-scene* and arguably the less discriminate 'eye' of the camera, which cannot help but afford us a sense of an omniscient perspective, even while it is depicting the view point of a single character" (Imelda 11).Deepa Mehta while undertaking this task of transforming Sidhwa's novel into a film *Earth* has to take into account *mise-en-scene* in place of point of view; a daunting task for any adaptor. The film maker has to follow the rule of inclusion and exclusion keeping in minds the theme, characterization, motif, time, economy and mood to create a desired effect. As the media shifts from textual to visual, the focus also shifts to angles, shots, lighting, sound and transition. All these combine to influence the audience's perception and understanding. *Ice-Candy-Man* from where the movie *Earth*'s inspired has a vast canvas on which Sidhwa delineated so many characters, representing different communities, religions, customs, cultures and creed with the touch of her brilliance.

Atypical Roles for Sidhwa's Women

Sidhwa's women characters in one way or the other try to challenge the age old patriarchy. Though they are the victims of subjugation but they possess admirable feminine power. The atrocities, barbarity, emotional turmoil, an acute sense of insecurity, individual weaknesses of women are depicted very faithfully. Being a Parsi, Sidhwa sat on a fence and took the side of neither Hindus nor that Muslims. She was an impartial observer. Sidhwa's 277 paged novels is squeezed by Mehta in less than two hours movie, making it almost impossible to capture every detail of words into images. But both Sidhwa and Mehta are the artists striving for a common cause-representation of women. Both are armed with different tools. Mehta in her film is not as explicit as Sidhwa is in representing women. In the film *Earth* women are subjected to all types of extreme cruelty in the wake of nationalistic chauvinism while Sidhwa's representation of women has wider connotation. She explores it beyond nationalist frenzy. Her women characters are aware and confidant of their individuality. They cannot be subjugated. Lenny, Ayah, Godmother and mother affirm their independent selfhood and demonstrate their resilience and refuse to yield. Deepa somehow lags behind Sidhwa in expressing the wider aspect of feminism. The film focuses more on showing how the fervour of nationalism and the violence is used and misused against women. Woman's body is used to fulfill the men's pride and honour. Sidhwa being a Parsee sat on a fence and held a neutral position during partition. She acted like an impartial spectator to Hindu-Muslim divide. But Deepa being a Hindu, born in Amritsar, makes her film in Hindi and targeting more to Hindu audience with both emotional and commercial limitations. Politically both the novel well as the film are inclined slightly towards Pakistan and India respectively. However, as far as the representation of women is concerned both the artists are impartial beyond doubts.

Earth Reduces the Larger issue of Sexuality to Violence

It is Lenny, the protagonist of the novel who narrates the whole story of partition stained in violence. She witnessed not only the barbarity, exploitation and brutalities inflicted on women but also observe the emotional, religious, political and historical drama of riot in the history of mankind personally. As a child she could understand the man's lascivious debasing attention towards women. The woman is merely reduced as an object of man's sexual gratification.

Ice-Candy-Man in fact, a saga of women's exploitation, suppression and marginalization in the male dominated patriarchal society. *Ice-Candy-Man* exposes how man falls to the level of beasts to establish his masculine power. On the other hand, the novel depicts the resilience and endurance the women demonstrated during the time of untold adversity. Ayah is inflicted pain by the man, who once loved her. The faith and love both are burnt in the fire of partition. In partition literature, women are represented as objects to be subjected to violence. The novel highlights women characters in their individual self. Each women, be it Shanta (Ayah), Lenny, her mother, or Godmother they represent way of life through different voices. The novel has strong women characters who resist masculine dominance in one form or the other. They are not passive but assertive in handling the situation with individual courage. Sidhwa choosing Lenny, as the narrator of the novel is quite a bold step. She describes the brutality of partition with chilling veracity. Like the author, Lenny is stricken with polio and is extremely observant narrator though at times her understanding is limited by her childlike innocence. As Jahanzeb Jahan comments:

> Bapsi Sidhwa delicately threads the story of an 8 year old girl named Lenny with the din of violence ready to crash around her world as the partition moves from political planning to reality. The story is told in the present tense as the events unfold before the young girls' eyes though moments of an older Lenny looking back are apparent.(slideshare.net/jahanzebjahan)

By making Lenny the narrator, Sidhwa displayed undaunting faith in her own sex. She took the side of women she was representing in her novel.

Dehumanization of Female Body in Both the Novel and the Film

Sidhwa and Mehta both show that women are dehumanized by men folk on their bodies – both during love and anger. In the novel, Lenny gives an account of how men-from beggars to holy men to British soldiers-gaze over Ayah's beautiful body. For this characteristic – Ayah's body becomes a symbol of undivided India – luring both insiders and outsiders with its bounty of treasures. In *Earth* the greedy male gaze towards Ayah's body and its symbolic connection to the physical territory of undivided India is beautifully captured at the park scene where male admirers from three different religions (Hindu, Muslim, and Sikh) sit circling around Ayah. In *Ice-Candy-Man*, Sidhwa describes the heart wrenching account of Ranna's village. Pir Pindo. The village was infested with sword wielding burly Sikhs. Ranna is torn apart from his mother and forced to hide in a small room packed with men and boys of his village. The Sikhs have attacked at least five villages around Dehra Mistri. Describing the incidence Sidhwa writes:

> They are like swarms of locusts, moving in marauding bands of thirty and forty thousands. They are killing Muslims. Setting fires, looting, parading the Muslim women naked through the streets-raping and mutilating them in the center of the village and mosques. The Bias, flooded by melting snow, and the monsoon, is carrying hundreds of corpses. There is an intolerable stench where the bodies, caught in the bends, have piled up. (ICM 197)

Ranna's account of Sikh attack in his village is nerve-wrecking. Ranna's account about his sister Khatija is heart tearing. Describing the scene Ranna witnessed, Sidhwa writes:

> No one minded the semi-naked specter as he looked in doors with his knowing, wide-set peasant eyes as men copulated with wailing children-old and young women... He saw babies, snatched from their mothers, smashed against walls and their howling mothers brutally raped and killed. (ICM 207)

Women were the worst victim, their bodies dehumanized, brutally mutilated and disfigured in this time of politico-religious frenzy. Amid this chaos, women are the common victims on both sides of the border irrespective of religion and community. Rape is a device used to de-humanize women. Sidhwa describes ruthless incidents of Ranna's village where all men were killed instantly, but women are kept alive to be raped again and again. Describing about these rape incidents, Jessica Islam and AnweshaMamtaz state thatthe rapes during partition were not originated from lust or carnal desire but rather from the idea of degrading the weaker "other" (women) to leave impact on the stronger "other" (men). By raping, mutilating and impregnating women, the purity of the bloodline of a particular community can be tempered.All this was done in the name of martyrdom and religion. The women who survived the rapes during riots were abandoned by their own people including their husbands, brothers and fathers. Describing one such incident about the pathetic condition of these women Sidhwa writes:"One cold night Lenny was awakened by a hideous wail. She asks Hamada,"Why do they wail and scream at night?""Poor fate-smitten woman," says Hamida, sighing. "What can a sorrowing woman do what wail?"(ICM213).Sidhwa also delineates in detail the terror and agony being inflicted on children also. A full chapter is devoted to describe the child Ranna's horrible tale of misery.

But Mehta's *Earth* skips Ranna's tale of woe. The film captures the tale of only one locality because of the time limitation a film goes through while the novel narrates all the incidents in detail. In the film, Ranna's tale of woe is restricted to a conversation between Lenny and cousin talking to some unnamed little boy about discovering the body of his naked mother. However, chapter 25 of the novel describes in detail Ranna's tale of woe. But both novel and the film yearn to convey the same message. Both the novel as well as film represents the subjugation of women during critical period of partition. In*Earth* we witness the greedy male gaze towards Ayah's body.

Mehta was carried away by the book *Ice-Candy-Man* in such a way that she wrote the script even be-fore sign-ing the con-tract. That was how Sidhwa wanted it to be: the director had to love her book deeply. At the same time, it was not al-ways easy to collaborate. Sidhwa was al-ways present when the film was being shot; she saw when her title was changed, she knew Mehta was making her trilogy on the natural elements (*Fire*, *Earth*, *and Water*). What was really difficult to accept was to see entire section of the book being deleted: once again, though, Sidhwa understood that cin-ema is a different media: for in-stance, it could not contain all the novel's incidents and characters. The most evident changes relate to the 'end': the novel *Ice-Candy-Man* gives a detailed account following the af-ter-maths of the Partition; whereas *Earth* fin-ishes soon after the event, when Ayah is kidnapped. Because of these differences what was becoming clear in their collaboration was that literature and cin-ema are different. Experience of read-ing the novel and of watch-ing the film are different.

Ending of the Novel and the Film

Unlike Sidhwa, Mehta kept Parsees completely meek and impartial. The film ends abruptly without the rescue of Ayah, leaving the audience to worry about the terrible fate Ayah befalls. The spectators come out of the cinema hall thinking about Ayah. She was not to be rescued in the film; therefore the character of Godmother was deleted from the film. Godmother is the great source and facilitator of female resistance in the novel. Wiping out Godmother from the film certainly raises the question of fidelity to the original text. The film is not an exact copy of the novel. Despite all this, a credit must be given to Deepa Mehta for keeping the plot intact. It kept the basic spirit of the novel intact. Sometimes director uses his own imagination and simply takes a novel as a jumping-off point. At others he may copy the original novel in a dogged way and yet fail to capture the true spirit of the original novel. Echoing similar views Macdonald and Macdonald observe: "A film can be faithful to the details and totally empty of the author's wit, irony, satire and meaning" (4). However, Mehta's film is other way round. It captured the true spirit of the novel despite having made certain changes. Fidelity is not the only criteria to evaluate a film transformed from the novel. Critics do stress on the fidelity concern but the film scholar Brian Macfarlane argues differently. Pointing out at this issue he says, "fidelity ...cannot profitably be used as an evaluative criterion; it can be no more than a descriptive term to designate loosely a certain kind of adaptation" (194).

Film adaption sometimes demands temporal changes as well. Novel ends with Ayah's firm resistance and Ice-candy-man's madness. Ayah's indifference to *Ice-Candy-Man* is a great example of women's resistance. "Ayah behaves as if he is invisible"(ICM 261).When he murmurs a couplet by Ghalib"My passion has brought me to your street – Where can I now find the strength to take me back?"Ayah behaves as if he is inaudible too (ICM 276). While consoling Ayah, Godmother tries to persuade her by saying that what's happened has happened and since he has married to her she must make the best of things. But Ayah, who represents the very core of feminine self-esteem and resilience says, 'I will not live with him' (ICM 261). Her firm resolve not to forget what has happened shows the true spirit of women's sense of birth and pride. She represents the resistance of a woman who was wronged by the man who once loved her. Religion and politics seem to dominate love and emotion. Patriarchal strength is tested on women's body. Ayah becomes the victim of patriarchal forces. She was raped and pushed into prostitution. And we come to know that she has been rechristened Mumtaz from Shanta by the *Ice-Candy-Man.*

Exploitation of Women by Women

However, in *Ice-Candy-Man* we come across the exploitation of slave-sister by Godmother (Rodabai). Slavesister is humiliated time and again by the woman who is the champion of feminist core. Slavesister's humiliation in presence of others in any case is unpleasant. She is leading a life of bonded slave. She is forced to suppress herself in every little conversation. She is not allowed to express herself. What is the significance of this relationship of Godmother and Slavesister? From the structural point of view it serves too little a purpose. But through this relationship, Sidhwa wants to convey an important message. She wants to bring all types of exploitations which normally lie hidden. To her, any type of suppression, manipulation and exploitation of women is worth exposing. Slavesister's exploitation conveys the readers that women also do not lag behind in exploiting women. This makes Sidhwa's feminist viewpoint broader, fairer and more receptive. In a true sense, Sidhwa's *Ice-Candy-Man* is essentially a feminist text. She brings women to the nucleus of the society. All women protagonists are presented realistically. All her women characters, be it Lenny, Ayah, Godmother, Slave sister and Mother, all raise consciousness among women in society and are the embodiments of feminine perception. Literature is an influential means of communication in the hands of writers to expose the excrescences prevailing in the society in various forms.

Novel versus Film: *Ice-Candy-Man* and *Earth*

Film came almost a decade later than the novel. In the span of ten years lot many things happen in the social, political, cultural and economic spheres. Novel gives the detail of pre-partitioned life of Lahore. It reveals the theme of partition slowly and surely. Sidhwa beautifully brings together the domestic life of a Parsi family the harrowing drama of horror, riots and massacres of 1947. *Ice-Candy-Man*is wonderful narrative which brings the communal violence to the surface from a girl's point of view. But the film goes straight to the rumours about partition. Mehta's adaptation of *Ice-Candy-Man* into *Earth* makes many interesting additions as well as omissions. It cannot be denied that certain omissions become essential to translate a novel to the screen due to the difference between written as opposed to visual and auditory media. While Sidhwa's novel comprises of nearly 277 pages, the screenplay for the film had to be shortened to fit the 101 minutes feature film length. In her selection, Mehta excludes certain female characters such as Slavesister, Godmother, Electric Aunt and Hamida. Lenny is the narrator and hence, interpreter of everything in the novel, but the film does not accord her that status. Many instances like Lenny's frequent visits to the house of Godmother, her conversation with Gandhiji, the mother's use of petrol to help move women across the border are completely absent in *Earth*. A whole section called "Ranna's story" which describes the bodily suffering of a Muslim boy and occupies substantial importance in the novel, is reduced to an insignificant short narrative by a nameless boy at the camp in the film. Mehta excludes some other characters, but retains some of their scenes and assigns those to other characters, i.e. Masseur gives Ayah a ride in his cycle in place of Sharbat Khan, Ice-candy-man threatens to drop Lenny suspended from the air instead of her brother Adi, etc. Making of film certainly involves commercial aspect also. Every innovation is governed by the laws of marketplace. The director has to meet the requirements of the mode of industrial production. The film is also subjected to the laws of profit making. It must entertain the audience. It has to reach millions to make profit where a novel can sell 20000 copies to make substantial profit. The director has to keep in mind the co-operative demands of the film production. For an effective screen writing one requires a knack for literature.

The novel '*Ice-Candy-Man* 'deals with several themes and is least concerned with its commercial success. Although the film '*Earth* 'sticks to the novel from where it is inspired, it is not exact cinematic rendition of the original. The film has taken into consideration an elaborate apparatus of the studios, production crew, musical aspect, the profit motive, official and unofficial censorship imposed by society as well by Government. The huge responsibility of catering to the public demand.

Parallels Between *Ice-Candy-Man* and *Earth*

Despite having used different medium of expression, both Sidhwa and Deepa attained similar results. They are the artists of common goal. Both the artists give voice to the female victims during partition. Both focus on feminine point of view. During the partition of 1947, largest number of people who were uprooted from their homes, mainly women. In the novel as well as in the film women are at the centre. Both Sidhwa and Mehta are transnational artists. Sidhwa belongs not only to Pakistan, India and the US but to the world. So does Deepa Mehta, as Richard Phillip her interviewer writes about her that she isa citizen filmmaker of the world. Not an Indian, not a Canadian either.

Though she was born in Am-rit-sar, moved with her family to New Delhi where she grad-u-ated in Phi-los-o-phy, cur-rently lives in Canada and belongs to the world.

Both the novel and the film i.e. *Ice-Candy-Man*and *Earth* share several similarities. Stating about Sidhwa and Mehta, Claudia Meoli says that the collaboration between the two is interesting not only because they share the same topics, interests and poetic expressions, but because they are both exiled artists. Both are exiled but have not been forced to leave their countries.Both Sidhwa and Mehta are the champion of women's cause. They have immense respect for each other. Both are inspired by the other's work. The partition of India is the key theme of both the novel as well as the film. Both could not keep their eyes shut to the 1947 partition which resulted in the world's biggest human migration accompanied by ethnic violence, kidnappings, killings and rapes. Both championed for women's cause but with different tools. While the former uses the flair of her pen and latter the magic of her camera.

Chapter-II

Reading *Water* as Film and Novel

> I'm not naïve. I know that films are very powerful. But I certainly don't say, 'I' m going to make a film that has social message', or 'Because 'I'm coloured or 'I'm a woman it has to be this way, otherwise it might be misinterpreted.' I want to be free to explore everything, even something that doesn't make me look good. If I want to explore it has to come from a place of honesty and not what is expected of me because I happen to be non-white or a woman –*Deepa Mehta.*

The film *Water* (2005) is one such example which is made with utmost honesty and hard work of Deepa Mehta. Devyani Saltzman in her book '*Shooting Water*' writes about the film: "Water was the final film in what would come to be known as the Elements Trilogy. Set in the holy city of Benares in 1938, the film follows the lives of almost invisible group of women in Indian society – Hindu widows" (6). The making of *Water* was an incredible effort on the part of Mehta. The script of the film was written by her in Toronto. Revealing the secret of her mother's hard work Devyani Saltzman says:

> Water was written at the kitchen table in my mother's little Victorian house in Toronto. On the night I would go for

> sleep over, I would wake up and come downstairs to find her sitting at the table with a cup of Earl Grey tea, a pack of Rothmans cigarettes, and a spiral-bound Hilroy notebook. She had often been there for many hours, writing. (8)

Mehta burnt the midnight oil to write the script of the film. But the real challenge came when Mehta started shooting the film in Banaras. The film was vehemently opposed by Hindu fundamentalists and was stopped before it could start. Not born to be defeated, Mehta made the film in Sri Lanka in 2005 under the title *Full Moon* with a new star cast. The film was released in 2005 and was admired by the film fraternity across the globe. One such admirer was Bapsi Sidhwa. She was so impressed by the film that she decided to write a novel based on this. One year later after the release of the film *Water* she wrote *Water* the novel inspired from the film. It was very unusual to write a novel based on the film. In this regard, Anita Joshua asserts:

> Working the other way round, Bapsi Sidhwa has penned a novel based on the film script. A telling story on the state of widows in India during colonial days, Water explores the ills of the prevailing social order. Seen through the eyes of an eight-year-old widow, the narrative brings out the travails of the widowhood in crystal clear clarity. (6)

This uncommon practice of writing a novel based on the film script is called 'Novelization'. Some even wonder whether this type of a study ever exists. Very few people believe that this type of literary activity exists. As Alex Suskind says that if you were unfamiliar with the world of novelizations, your immediate reaction is that their existence is likely one of incredulity. This literary activity is also old but not as old as an adaptation. But novelization of the film into novels has existed for almost as long as the film themselves. We know that ever since the birth of films, they have been relying heavily on literary sources especially novels. The reasons for this may be that the material already exists for the film maker. They believe that some success has already been achieved by the novel and the most important reason may be is to widen the sphere of reach the film may achieve by becoming available to illiterate spectators too. All great classics have been transformed into films. Usually filmic sources are off springs of fictional sources. But Sidhwa's transmuting a film into a novel is the other way round.

Transforming a film (a visual text) into a novel (literary text) is a rarer activity but it too has a history of about hundred years to its credit. It began with silent films like *Sparrows* (1926) and *London after Midnight* (1927) which were transformed into the novels. Talking about the beginning of novelization, Makhlknech Johannes writes, "...Blockbuster like *King Kong* (2005), dir. Peter Jackson), *The Wolfman* (2010, dir. Joe Johnston) and *Cowboys and Aliens* (2011, dir. John Favreau) all have their novelistic alter ego" (21). Expressing similar views about this trend in Hollywood, Kent and Joe Gotler write "In the past three decades they have become a regularly used tool for promotion of many of Hollywood's major cinematic releases – a calculated means of maximizing profit" (94).

The first film which received the book treatment was the 1933 classic film *King Kong*. The original black-and-white film version of *King Kong* was released in 1933and novelization of original *King Kong* came in 1932 as a part of films' advance marketing strategy. It was written by Delos W. Lovelace though credited to Edgar Wallace and Marian C. Cooper. Thereafter in 1970s, the films like *Star War* and *Alien* were transformed into the novels and millions of copies were sold. It was the time when films were released in the theatres only. Films almost died after their releases. The best way to re-live a film is to have it written in a book format. Novelization makes us remember the experience we once experienced. Katy Wild, the editorial director of Titan Publishing Group Ltd. says that people just want to see it as other element of the entertainment. But there is no dearth of people who regard novelization as a work for hire and hatch-work. Mel Gilden says, "Generally, novelizations are considered to be the scum of literature"(melgilden.co). It is regarded as a low grade literary phenomenon. But both adaptation and novelization are based on the idea of transformation. Arguing about film and fiction, Keith Cohen, a film scholar, says that the film and fiction go through "dynamics of exchange" (92). The exchange of film to fiction and vice-versa. Former gives emphasis in "showing" while the later stresses on "telling." In simple words novelization is novel based on a film. Eliciting about the difference between two mediums, Seymour Chatman in his essay writes:

> A close study of film and novel versions of the same narrative reveals with great clarity the peculiar powers of the two media. Once we grasp those peculiarities, the reasons for the differences in form, content, and impact of the two versions strikingly emerge. (404)

The idea behind this intertextuality is to produce variety but Linda Hutcheon has a contrary opinion, she writes: "…In all forms of adaptations, repetition is seemingly as desired a factor as variation. With novelization, repetition is arguably more important than variation" (3). What she wants to argue is that novelization involves more of repetition than of variety and copiousness. Jonathan Coe goes a step further by attributing this genre as "that bastard, misshapen offspring of the cinema and the written word, [Novelization is] execrably–written texts: cheap, hastily assembled adaptations of recent movies and T.V. series" (jonathancoewritten.com). Writing about transferring the film *Water* into a Novel of Sidhwa, Anu says that it was for the first time that she came across a novel which has been based on a film. Usually, it isother way round; Books inspire film makers to make movies, following their creativity, added much needed spices to transform a good written story into commercial viable cinematic experience. Contrary to this, commenting about the source material of films, Paul Wells in his essay 'Thou Art Translated' writes:

> Since the very beginning of cinema, literature has provided an extra ordinary range of source materials for film texts. Writing about this relationship has been fundamentally preoccupied with the ways in which 'the word'-something you read-becomes the image-something you see-raising issues about the very nature and effect of 'adaptation' itself, as narrative moves from the primary text into the realm of the visual. (199)

Though rare, yet transmutability of texts is not one way. Commenting on film and literature Roland Barthes writes: "The cultural codes [deployed by any single story] … will emigrate to other texts, there is no lack of host" (205). What he means to say is that there is every possibility of inter-change of one medium to another and vice-versa. He emphasized that the very hypothesis of narrative is based on transmutability. This chapter contains a wide range of issues, each focusing on certain aspects of novelization with special reference to *Water* the film by Deepa Mehta and its consequent novelization by Sidhwa. Discussing the process of turning a film script into novel, Sidhwa herself says:

> "I have never worked so hard, but it was for me a new and exhilarating experience." In case of writing *Water*, she said, "the plot and characters were already there, but I had to

> bring the skeletal script and cinematic images to life with words. Besides being a gripping story, the plot deals with subject close to my heart-that of the oppressive hold of tradition on women, in this case, religious tradition. It tells of oppression and the constraints that govern even a girl – child's life in a patriarchal society. I have always been active in women's issues. (Redhotcurry.com)

Writing a novel based on a film is not a mean task. Famous novelization writer, Foster says that it's always amusing, you take a book, say, *To Kill a Mocking Bird* (1960), throw away three quarters of it and win an Academy Award for best adapted screenplay. But if you take a screenplay and add three quarters of original material to it – which is a much, much more difficult piece of writing-well, that's by definition 'hackwork.' It was much harder, having done both, to the screen plays and makes a book out of that [to] take a terrific book and make a screenplay out of it. He implies that novelization is far more difficult than adaptation. Despite this, novelization has a stigma about it. He goes on to say that to some it sounds like an insult. The writer of the novelizations has to watch the film again and again. Alex Irvine while writing a novel for the film *Pacific Rim* (2013) got to see the movie and had a long conversation with the director Guillermo del Toro about the story and plot. In the present chapter the focus centers on the proposed texts; the film *Water* by Mehta and the novel *Water* by Sidhwa. Both of them are the artists of immense talent having a very high reverence for each other and their works. Both are genuinely concerned about the women.

Reading of the Film *Water*

The focus of attention shifts to study film *Water* by Mehta and then to the novel *Water* by Sidhwa. The film *Water* is written and directed by Deepa Mehta and is produced by David Hamilton in the year 2005. It is the third of Mehta's elemental trilogy, followed by *Fire*(1996) and *Earth* (1998). Speaking about her Elemental Trilogy and *Water*, Mehta herself says that the film is set in the 1930s and is about the politics of religion and its impact on ordinary people. '*Fire*'is about the politics of sexuality and *Earth* is about politics of nationalism and *Water* about the politics of religion. The theme of the film is about politics of religion. It explores how religion is used, misused and distorted by the people to suit it for their own benefits. "Water is a dark introspect into the tales of rural Indian widows in the 1930s and covers controversial subjects such as misogyny and ostracism" (filmisl and.net).

Making of the Film *Water*

Making of the film *Water* needs to be first discussed. The film *Water* is set in the pre-independence decade of 1930s in the year 1938 in Rawalpur, a village on the Bihar-Bengal border. It is a poignant and heart wrenching commentary on the pathetic plight of Indian widows at an ashram in Varanasi, India – especially child widows – in the late 1930s. The film addresses a very ancient Hindu tradition of widow-burning at the funeral pyre of her dead husband. Commenting on this pathetic tradition of widowhood Manju Jaidka writes:

> The picture of the sordid lives of the widows is presented through a series of binaries, contrasting the various lots of those who control the society and those who are controlled. At the receiving end is the unfortunate community of social outcasts whose fault is that its members have outlived their spouses.(59)

The film by Mehta signifies the dual aspect of Indian culture symbolically through water. *Water* connotes purity and also denotes annihilation. The film was released in 2005, last film of the trilogy, addressing the plight of widows in Indian society. It is a poignant story of Indian conservative society of pre-independence era. The film presents the squalid and disreputable life widows spend in ashrams. The film is based on a Manuscript, an ancient Hindu text which says a woman is half dead after her husband's death. After the death of her husband a widow is left with three choices: she can throw herself on the funeral pyre of her husband and die with him; she can marry his brother, if available; or she has to lead a life of complete isolation and seclusion. The third option forces her to enter in the ashram. She has to wear white clothes, in some cases to shave her head and live in constant mourning to atone for her husband's death. They are regarded as social outcasts. Devyani Saltzman, daughter of Deepa Mehta's writes about the film in her book *'Shooting Water'*:

> Water was the final film in what would come to be known as the Elements Trilogy. Set in the holy city of Benares in 1938, the film follows the lives of an almost invisible group of women in Indian society-Hindu widows. Women whose religion prescribed that they atone for their husband's death by living as ascetics, wearing only white, the colour of mourning, shaving their heads to renounce vanity, and living in ashrams, or spiritual refuges. Hindu widows practiced a different form of wifely devotion from the more widely known sati, in which a woman would throw herself on her husband's funeral pyre, burning herself to death. (6)

Commenting about this ancient sacred Hindu text she further says: "The *Manuscript,* one of the sacred Hindu texts, explains that in life a woman is half of her husband and therefore, in the event of his death, she is half-dead. The practice of ascetic widowhood still exists in India" (6). To her utter surprise, this brutal practice still exists even after the fifty years of independence. In order to understand it comprehensibly, the argument starts with the making of the film by Mehta and its consequent transformation into the novel of same name by Sidhwa. Let the discussion start with the making of the film.

The film *Water* had its roots from an idea which came to Mehta in 1993 while shooting a film in Benares. Describing this episode Devyani writes:

> My mother told me the idea for *Water* came to her while they were shooting in Benares in 1993. While she sat on the ghats on an early morning before shooting, she noticed an elderly woman dressed only in white, descending into the river for morning prayers. A production assistant explained to her that she was a Hindu widow, waiting to attain 'Kashi moksha' – liberation from the cycle of life, death and rebirth – which can instantly be gained by dying in the holy city of Benares. (6)

Based on the idea she worked hard to write the script of the film. It was beautifully crafted by her. Describing about the script Devyani writes:

> The script was beautiful, set against the backdrop of India's struggle for independence from the British. It follows the lives of three Hindu widows living in an ashram: Shakuntala, a middle aged woman hardened by her fate; Kalyani, a beautiful twenty-year-old, prostituted out to wealthy clients as one of the only means by which the ashram can earn an income; and Chuyia, a feisty child-widow of eight. (6)

This story motivated Mehta to make the film *Water*. The film had a budget of 2 million Canadian Dollars, almost one thirteenth of the average Hollywood film. The making of *Water* was not an easy task. The film got into controversy even before its start. Making of *Water* was extremely tough. Mehta has raised the issue of religious hypocrisy in this film. As James Mottram reveals that originally it was due to be shot in February 2000. It is the story of widows in 1930s India. But the Government revoked shooting orders one day before filming was due to begin. Worse still, death threats were issued to Mehta and actors by protesting Hindu fundamentalists.

After acquiring all necessary permissions from the NDA (National Democratic Alliance) Govt. in Delhi led by Atal Bihari Bajpei. The script was sent to Ministry of Information and Broadcasting (I& B). It was approved without any cuts. The shooting gear arrived in Banares a couple of days in advance. Everything was running as per plan. The film was to be shot on Arrilex BL5 camera with 35mm Kodak film stock. The earlier cast of the film was ready with Urvi (Chuyia) and Shabana Azmi (Shakuntala) who were later dropped from the cast. On the day, the shooting was to start and the first scene was to shoot Urvi playing for Chuyia, an unruly mob of about 75 people, women, wearing saris, raising their arms high in the air shouting slogans 'GANGA MAILE NAHIN KAROGE! GANDA PANI GANGA NAHIN SAHEGI!' stormed into the set destroying it. These campaigns were led by the protestors belonging to Hindu right wing RSS, VHP and Shiv Sena. They accused Deepa for maligning Indian Culture. "In their opinion there was no need to tell the world of the problems of widows in India and Mehta was simply being opportunistic, looking for a story that would sell in the West" (brightlightsfilm.com).

They shouted 'WATER PICTURE MURDABAD! DEEPA MEHTA MURDABAD!' The crowd yelled to see the film as well Mehta dead. The shooting was stopped on day one itself. But the film management decided to shoot Urvi (Chuyia's) head shaven on the back garden of the hotel instead of shooting in the city.

Next morning as Urvi Gokani was ready in the hotel garden constructed as Manikaranika Ghat, camera rolled and the action started. Describing this incident Deyani says that as the barber pulled out a flip-razor to begin shaving, sounds started to fill the garden, rolling over the flower beds from the direction of the road. An unruly mob chanting slogans 'WATER PICTURE MURDABAD! DEEPA MEHTA MURDABAD!' stormed in, burning down the sets and throwing the pieces into the Ganges. The film crew watched all this in utter silence. Devyani writes about the incidence: "We watched in silence as the flames licked the edges of the film set, like the pyres of Manikarnika" (68).All the national news channel flashed 'Breaking News. "The sets of Deepa Mehta's *Water* had been burned and thrown into the Ganges by angry protesters, accusing her of defiling Hinduism and polluting the holy river. Footage of our wooden sets was shown in flames on Assi Ghat and in the *galis* behind it" (Saltzman 68).Similarly writing about the incident, Amrita Basu writes. "There were widespread protests as the conservative section of the society viewed it as the contamination of India and Indian Womanhood by Western Imperialism" (6).

The Hindu-fundamentalists thought that the film is going to distort Indian Culture. BJP, RSS, VHP and Shiv Sena people vehemently opposed the film. They considered the film as an attack on the culture and traditions of Varanasi. Mehta recalls that it was very scary, how people were arbitrarily reinterpreting the rules regarding culture. Death threats were issued against Deepa Mehta and she was declared as whore and anti-Hindu. Sensing a great financial loss, Ajay Virmani, the financer was desperate to pull out of this project and the film. As their protest took an ugly shape, Ajay Virmani fearing loss of 700000 Canadian Dollars, pulled out of the film and left Mehta in the lurch. The film came to a grinding halt before it could start. Yuen Carrucan describes this incident:

> There was never any arrests made over the vandalism that the film sets suffered when the protests began, yet Deepa Mehta was threatened with arrest for aiding an attempt at suicide and was forced to leave Varanasi. The crew was also advised by the government to leave the city immediately, as our safety could not be guaranteed. (brightlightsfilm.com)

The star cast of the film was: Shakuntala (Shabana Azmi), Kalyani (Nandita Das), Chuyia (Urvi Gokani), Gulabi (Raghuvir Yadav), Manorama (Madhumati), Sadanad (Kulbhushan Kharbanda), Narayan (John Abraham), Waheeda Rehman (Narayan's Mother),Vinay Pathak . The music for the featured songs is given by A.R. Rehman and the lyrics by Sukhwinder Singh and Raqueeb Alam. The songs are composed by Javed Akhtar. The background score of the film is composed by Mychael Diana.The cinematography is done by Giles Nuttgens. Anurag Kashyap has translated the script from English to Hindi, the final editing is done by Colins Morrie and the final print runs 114 minutes. But before the film could start, it was stopped. Not to be out done, Deepa was rock solid not to abandon the project at any cost. In 2004, she started the film again with new location, new name and some new faces.

Re-birth of *Water* as *Full Moon*

Four years since *Water* had been shut down in India, the film resurrected from scratch with new locale and some new faces. Urvi Gokani was replaced by Sarla Kariayawasam, Nandita Das by Lisa Ray and Shabana Azmi by Sima Biswas. Sri Lanka was selected a new alternative location. Writing about the new location Devyani writes: "The lush foliage and rivers could pass for rural

India without the threat from Hindu right...The money had been raised from the scratch after the losses of Benares" (151). Deepa has to buy her script back from Ajay, who was the earlier financer and owned the rights. This time Canadian Government, through Tele film Canada, a film funding body, provided the investment for the film. It was great gesture by any country to support its artists. Tele film Canada made it mandatory to make the film in Canada's two official languages, French and English. The final funding of the film came through Mark Burton, a Los Angeles-based producer, an owner of Echo Lake Productions. With a budget of, 5.7 million Canadian dollars the film started in Sri-Lanka with changed name *Full Moon*, a name nobody would question, with a new cast. This unique and silly-sounding name was suggested by David.

During the course of four years Nandita who was to play Kalyani, a beautiful young widow, no longer possessed the charm and deep innocence needed for the character of Kalyani. She was replaced by Lisa Ray, the star of *Bollywood/Hollywood*. Mehta felt that because of Shabana's high profile and political stature she might endanger the secrecy of film's re-production in Sri-Lanka and it might put the film's release in jeopardy. Shabana was replaced Sima Biswas, a very fine actress from Assam, who worked in theatre and has starred Shekhar Kapoor's *Bandit Queen*. She was chosen to play the role of Shankuntala. Urvi, who was to play Chuyia, was now a twelve year old girl and was too big for the part.She lacked the innocence of an eight year old child widow. Sarala from the suburb of Galle was selected for the role of Chuyia. She neither knew Hindi nor English. Selection of Sarala for the film is very interesting, describing it Saltzman writes in her book *Shooting Water:*

> Mom was disappointed, but since Sarala and her family had driven, four hours to see them, Mom decides to test her with

> one of Chuyia's harder scenes, when she is left at Ashram by her Baba, or father...Sarala listened to Mom explain the scene through a Sinhala translator. Direction through translation; it was crazy idea. But as soon the translator finished, Sarala immediately stood up, grabbed his legs as if he were Baba, and begin crying, telling him not to leave her . She spoke in Sinhala, but language seemed inconsequential. She possessed the spirit of Chuyia. (167)

This was how Chuyia was found. Mini-Benares was created with a Sri Lankan river as the Ganga. Temples, ghats, trees and natural landscape were incorporated into the set. Errol Kelly was the master set builder. He was the art director for *Indiana Jones* and the *Temple of Doom's*, Sri-Lankan unit under the direction of Steven Spielberg. Benares was recreated on the bank of a Sri-Lankan river. Hindu temple town was constructed by the plywood. It appeared like mini-Benares. Sri Lankan people helped Deepa in all possible ways. Suresh and Mandy a friendly couple offered their house as the house for Narayan's home. Despite all the hurdles, fearless Deepa with an eighty-person crew started shooting *Water* in Sri Lanka on Easter Sunday, the day of resurrection.The first scene was where Chuyia is brought by bullock cart to the river *ghats*. Describing the opening page of the film script Devyani Saltzman writes:

> CREDITS OVER: FADE IN:
> EXT.TROPICAL VISTA–DAY
>
> A green lush landscape, peppered with coconut trees and banana groves as far as the eye can see. CLOSE–UP of creaking wooden wheels as they enter the frame, fill it and then wipe it clean. We are behind a bullock cart as it plods along, its passengers hidden by their own long shadows. On

> two tiny, bare feet, encircled with silver anklets, dangling by the side of bullock cart. The small bells on the anklets ring sweetly as the feet swing back and forth to the easy rhythm on the cart. (189)

Chuyia (Sarla) revealed and thus begins *Water* again under the feigned title *Full Moon*. This time no elaborate religious ceremony was performed before the starting the film. Describing the first scene Devyani writes:

> As the assistant directors went to their positions around the vista, Dylan cleared us away from the cart. Sarala sat quietly, chewing on a piece of sugarcane given to her by the art department. Mom gave her direction and Kay translated it into Sinhala. ...'and…Action!" …The driver whipped the bullocks and the cart lurched forward. I fell back into the waiting crew and wondered how Mom felt as the cart moved slowly down the dirt track. How it felt to be reborn. (194-195)

This is how *Water* was born again in Sri Lanka. In a later scene, Sarala wearing a small white sari was shaven by a Sri-Lankan barber dressed like an Indian. As her previous film *Earth* is presented through the eyes of a girl Lenny, so is the film *Water* is presented through an eight year old widow Chuyia. As Manju Jaidka writes:

> The eight-year old child widow, Chuyiais dumped in widow's home when her aged husband passes away. At the ashram she shares her space with widows of various shades and colours: the obese Madhumati who is like a keeper of a brothel, ruling over the home with an iron hand; Kunti, Bua, and other aged widows who have long since reconciled to their lot; the younger Shakuntala, a strong but silent

> sufferer aware of the injustice in their lives but unable to do anything about it. There is also young and beautiful Kalyani, barely out of her teens, who is treated differently by the warden. She has a separate room for herself, is allowed to keep her hair long, and receives special gifts occasionally because she earns livelihood for all of them. (60)

The film is a poignant story of the widows in an ashram of Vrindaban. It depicts the double standard of Hindu priestly class. Brahmins do not hesitate to use their lofty social rank to exploit the vulnerable classes of society such as women, children and widows. *Water* was the last in the series of her elemental trilogy. *Fire* reveals the story of two married women ignored and neglected by their husbands. They fall in love with each other. *Earth* (1998) focused around how the relationship among Hindus, Muslims and Sikhs totter in the wake of partition and how the woman and her body is used to give vent to man's pride. *Water* is the last of the three and is the most poignant, set in colonial India against Gandhi's freedom struggle. This was the time when Gandhi's influence was visible everywhere. The film begins with a text from Manusmriti on the black screen. A stern warning garbed in a religious text appears on the screen. Explaining the meaning of the text which appears on the screen at the onset of the film, Wendy Doniger and Brian Smith writes:

> A virtuous wife who remains chaste when her husband has died goes to heaven just like those chaste men, even if she has no sons. But a woman who violates her (vow to her dead) husband because she is greedy for progeny is the object of reproach here on earth and loses the world beyond. No (legal) progeny are begotten here by another man or another man's wife; nor is second husband ever prescribed for virtuous women. A woman who abandons her own inferior

> (caste birth) man becomes an object of reproach in this world; she is said to be 'previously had by another man'. A woman who is unfaithful to her husband is an object of reproach in this world; (then) she is reborn in the womb of jackal and is tormented by the diseases born of her evil. (116)

The film was released on November 2005. Mehta offered her audience a movie of an immense quality. It is a movie having a global reach. Divulging about the message of the film, David Burton asserts:

> Mehta's principal message is that, although the film is set in 1930s, the mistreatment of the widows in India is an issue of pressing contemporary concern. She closes the film with the claim that " there are thirty four million widows in India according to 2001 census, and continue to live in conditions of social, economic and cultural deprivation as prescribed 2000 years ago by Sacred Texts of Manu," the ancient Hindu law book. (digitalcommos.unomaha.edu/jrf)

The film commences with this stern textual warning on the screen and the action starts with the sun rise. A bullock cart is carrying ailing Hira Lal, Chuyia's husband to die peacefully on the bank of the Ganga at Varanasi. Chuyia is sitting at the back of the cart, unaware, chewing a long piece of sugarcane. She was swinging her feet back and forth and the tiny bells encircling her tiny anklets jingled. She is wearing red blouse and a blue skirt. She had a little idea of where she was going and what this journey meant for her. She even tickled the sole of his foot, and it twitched slightly. As she repeated the action, she was reprimanded by her mother-in-law by striking her head with a fan. The bullock cart arrives at the bank of the Ganga. A boatman was waiting for them. He lifted Hira Lal and placed him in his boat. The boat picks up some speed and the small temples and domes came into view. Chuyia asks her father about the burning crimson flames. Finally, Hira Lal's fever-racked heart gave out and he dies. The film begins with the bullock cart journey whereas Sidhwa devotes 23 pages before arriving to this point. The novel begins with the Prologue, 1936 a Village on the Bihar-Bengal Border. Chuyia tired of playing with her clay dolls, goes in search of gooseberries, wandering deep into the forest in search of wild lychees, but finds Tun-Tun, an abandoned puppy.

Chapter-I of the novel gives a description of Bhagya sitting cross-legged on the kitchen floor grinding rice with a mortar and pestle. Somnath comes into the kitchen with what he thinks as good news. Revealing Bhagya that HiraLal's mother wants Chuyia to marry him. 'I have agreed,' he said. 'Their horoscopes match. We have to look at some auspicious dates. They want the marriage to take place before Diwali-in September or October. The monsoon will be over and our guest can sleep outside" (Water 6-7). Bhagya is shocked to hear this. "She is only six,' Bhagya said, her quavering voice was so low Somnath had to strain to catch her words. 'I've heard HiraLal is a grandfather'. 'He's younger than me, about forty -Somnath said. 'They don't want a dowry; they will pay for the wedding. She will be well cared for. HiraLal's mother is a kind woman. She will be good to our girl. 'Shouldn't you have consulted me? said Bhagya (Water 7).The manner Somnath takes the decision of his daughter's marriage reveals the male mind set. Somnath took a very important decision about his daughter's marriage without consulting his wife. And the reason behind the early marriage is also elaborated in the novel. Justifying his decision he says, "He is not bad-looking. The family is of noble Brahmin lineage" (Water 7). And Chuyia's mother could do nothing but wishes 'Eeshh, Bhagwan: may she never come of age!" (Water7). Such is the helplessness of a mother.

Unlike the film; the novel gives detail about the events prior to marriage. Due to time constraint film does not explain the reasons behind this marriage. Mehta could not clarify due to time limits in the film while Sidhwa reveals it in detail.

The Women Protagonists in Film as Well as in the Novel

Both in the film as well as in the novel there are three important female protagonists. Chuyia is one of them. She is a child widow. Chuyia (Sarla Kariyawasam), an eight year-old child bride is told by her father that the husband she has never met has died. Consequently she has to accept the monastic life of an ashram. She has to live a life of deprivation, devotion, purity and prayer. Kalyani (Lisa Rey), a young widow who is forced into prostitution in order to support the ashram is another woman protagonist. Shakuntla (Sima Biswas) is the third woman protagonist in the film as well as in the novel. Due to very narrow interpretations of Hinduism, widows are expected to live in poverty and chastity. In the background to their stories is the beginning of Mohandas Karam Chand Gandhi's campaign to drive the British out of India and establish an independent India movement through non-violence. The hope and progressive thinking that Gandhi introduced into Indian society provides a stark contrast to the sad and oppressive lives that widows must endure. Through the lives of the three main characters, *Water* exposes the appalling treatment meted out to women in India. Even today the Indian society is hostile to widows. Both the texts represent larger issues about how religion is misused by people in a position of power to deny human rights. In the ensuing discussion, an attempt is made to dive deep into the characters of women protagonists especially Chuyia, Kalyani and Shakuntala in both the texts (Novel &Fim).

Chuyia (Sarla Kariayawasam)

Chuyia (Sarla Kariayawasam) is the first of the three protagonists in the film *Water*. Sarla, who played Chuyia in the film, hails from Galle, Sri Lanka. She was the first Sri Lankan child artists to make an international debut. She was selected from out of fifty girls auditioned by Deepa Mehta. She was selected for the most challenging role of Chuyia-the child widow. Sarla, who did not speak a word in Hindi, learnt all dialogues by heart and acted in the film superbly and stunned the audience as well as critics. She did not hesitate to shave her head. In the film she played a widow, presenting an outdated, callous and rotten tradition of child marriage and widowhood. Her marriage is arranged by her father though the mother opposes meekly. As the film begins Chuyia is shown as a free and rebellious little girl. She is accompanying her dying husband on his last journey. Her introduction in the film is shown eating sugar cane and playing mirthfully with the feet of her dying husband as he is being transported in a bullock cart. She is completely ignorant of the situation she is going to face. Her playfulness is witnessed throughout the film. After the death of her husband she left in the widow ashram with most of the elderly widows. This ashram is run by Madhumati (Manorama), a stringent ruler. Explaining Chuyia about the religious duties of widows Madumati says: "In grief, we are all sisters here and this house is our refuge. Our Holy Books say, a wife is part of her husband while he is alive. Right? And when husbands die", she concludes the catechism, "wives also half die" (Water 42).To this Chuyia responds that means we are also half alive. Shouting at Madhumati, Chuyia yells, "I don't want to be a stupid widow! Fatty!" She said rightly and challenges the authority of Madhumati by disturbing the agonizing quiet of the ashram. She sets the ashram in tumult.

Even the corpse like widow, Paitrajji made up a bit of doggerel and sang:

> *Chuyia the mouse,*
> *With her sharp little teeth,*
> *And her tight little bite,*
> *Bled the lumpy old louse* (Water 45).

Such is the influence of Chuyia on the inmates of the ashram. She becomes the symbol of liberation. She is forced to wear white clothes. But her silence towards the end of the film is agonizing. The river Ganga is a symbol of purification for Hindus. Water is necessary for both physical and spiritual life. It is holy as well profane. Chuyia is tricked to fill the vacuum created by Kalyani's death and is thrown into prostitution. She becomes the victim of lusting hawks. As Manju Jaidka writes: "At the end of the film, she is nothing but an inert mass, violated, drugged and abused" (Water 63). But in the end Chuyia's escape from Varanasi in the arms of Narayan (John Abraham) is certainly relieving.

Chuyia (Sarla) is the best part of Water. She is cute, energetic and perfect choice for the role. In real life she cannot speak a word of Hindi. Her work in *Water* is complete memorization of the lives and their phonetic regurgitation. This makes her performance even more profound. What an amazing across! (data/data/com.android.com)

Water is traditionally a symbol of change and progression. The train is a force of modernity and progress that takes Chuyia and Narayan into Gandhi's new India and away from the oppressive traditions prevalent in Indian society.

Sidhwa's delineates the character of Chuyia through words. She is not bound by the constraints of time, space and budget. As we go through the novel, little Chuyia (Sarla) of the film seems to peep through the pages in the novel. She appears to talk to the readers, running, playing, jumping, fighting in the pages of the book. Sidhwa has drawn her character very well. And at times while watching the film it appears that film has been adapted from the novel no other way round.

Kalyani (Lisa Ray)

Kalyani is another young widow residing in the ashram. Her role is played by beautiful Lisa Ray, a Canadian actress, model and television host. "She is the prized possession of the ashram: the beautiful, young, fair-skinned Kalyani (Lisa Ray) who is allowed to keep her hair long and sleeps in special room on the second floor of the ashram" (hehefnet.com). She is a vision in her widows white. Only she is allowed to spare her hair as to look beautiful and attract customers. Describing her, Jeannette Catsouls writes:

> The limpid-eyed Kalyani (Lisa Ray) – the only widow whose head has not been shaved – is forced into prostitution by ashram's domineering housemother. Employing a sly eunuch as go-between, the housemother sells Kalyani's services to a wealthy Brahmin on the other side of the river. (The New York Times 28 April 2008)

A chance encounter with Narayan, who is a Gandhian, makes her believe about some possibility of marriage that would take her away from the life of ashram. But this is the India of 1930s. The re-marriage of widows is unthinkable. She displays a great courage to love Narayan and has the guts to fight against the tradition. She rebels against the rules and breaks the tradition. In this regard, Guadalupe Mora says, "Kalyani's leaving the place where all widows were, was a major turning point in the movie. She went against tradition and wants to fight for her love, Narayan" (internationalcinemaeducation.word-press). She is forced into prostitution by Madhumati (Manorma) to support the ashram.

Madhumati is an older widow who runs the ashram. Kalyani is the only bread winner of the ashram. She is an older version of Chuyia. Narayan falls in love with Kalyani and determines to save her. He was utterly enchanted by her beauty. He is spell bound by her beauty. But ironically his father has been using Kalyani as a prostitute. He is such an evil that after Kalyani he turns to Chuyia.When Kalyani comes to know that Seth Dwakanath is Narayan's father, she drowns herself. As she realized that she cannot marry Narayan, in an utter despair puts an end to her life.

After her death the void is created which needs to be filled to run the ashram. The economics of survival comes into play. The inmates of the ashram are to be fed and clothed. The only bread-winner, Kalyani is no more. The other fitting candidate is no other than an eight year child Chuyia. Mehta condemns not only religion but attacks the way it is used for economic and political gains. Kalyani is shown majestically in the film. She is strongly associated with blue colour, the colour of Lord Krishna. It is also the colour traditionally used to represent water. When Kalyani sneaks out to be with Narayan, the atmosphere in the film is tinged with blue background symbolizing purity and love that has developed between Narayan and Kalyani. The blue colour in the film symbolizes love which eventually will transform into spirituality.

Shakuntala (Seema Biswas)

Shakuntala (Seema Biswas) is another woman protagonist in the film. She is an enigmatic character. She is another widow in the ashram. She observes a sincere devotion to her faith. She is a sensitive middle aged widow who is like a mother figure for Chuiya. Though she plays a peripheral role in the film. The focus lies on Kalyani and Chuyia. But in the final scene she emerges as final protagonist. Chuyia and Kalyani stirred Shakuntala to ask question about her faith in religion as the film approaches to its end. She ensures a safe passage of Chuyia from Varanasi. She performs an act of kindness and generosity by saving Chuyia from Widow's ashram. Her act of defiance is also one of religious defiance against a set of powerful beliefs she had lived with her entire life. This culminates in the scene when she confronts the priest Sadananda (Kulbhushan Kharbanda) about the scriptures concerning widows. A sympathetic character, Sadananda explains that the relevant scriptures do list a life of self denial as one of the options for widows, along with being burnt with her husband or marrying the husband's younger brother. However, he also reveals that there are now new laws in favour of remarriage, but religious groups have ignored these laws since the laws do not suit them. This is a crucial scene in the film since it directly addresses the danger of religion having too much power and influence to the extent that it can bypass the law for its own end. It also exposes how religious beliefs can be hijacked to serve the needs of people in a position of authority. Thomas Caldwell says that Shakuntala's taking away Chuyia from the Ganges, symbolizes the progress.

Madhumati (Manorama)

Madhumati, another important character in the film, played by Manorama deserves attention. Not all the inmates of the ashram are exploited, Madhumati is an exploiter. The evil in the society is perpetrated not only by men but women too are responsible. Madhumati is one such example. She too joins the institution of patriarchy in exploiting women. She acts like a lazy but ruthless seal to demean women. But Sidhwa depicts her quite sympathetically. She delineates that Madhumati too is the victim of patriarchal forces. Not much has changed in Hindu society as exploitations of widows still exist in India. After having discussed the women characters, the focus shifts to study *Water* as a film in a broader perspective.

Reading of the film *Water*

Mehta adapted Sidhwa's *Ice-Candy-Man* for her brilliant film *Earth*, and here, Sidhwa adapts Mehta's controversial film *Water* into the novel of same name. Reading of a film text is different from reading a novel. Since both the media are constituted differently, both require to be analyzed differently. Film is a unique way of telling stories with moving images adorned with voice, sound and music. And decoding of a film is definitely a more challenging task. Film too is a communication tool. As we know film is multi-sensory and is replete with audio and visual details. This chapter focuses on to examine and analyze the film *Water* under the scanner of cinematic narrative. The struggle of widows is captured in the camera. They are portrayed against the socio-cultural, political and religious tradition.

The film is set in 1938 pre-Independent India in the backdrop of Gandhi's influence. The film is replete with spectacular visual multilayered narrative, like her earlier two films; *Fire* and *Earth* in her elemental trilogy. *Water,* the final film in Mehta's Trilogy takes on the issue of religious politics. In this regard, David Burton opines: "Mehta's film makes it clear that the male hegemony seeks to rationalize the mistreatment of widows by appealing to the authority of Hindu scripture; the film opens with a translation from The Laws of Manu which gives unambiguous construction about the dharma of a wife whose husband has died" (digitalcommos.unomaha.edu/jrf). The film takes on the issue of ancient concept of Sati. The Sati or "Virtuous woman" – the name given to a widow who burns or is forced to be burnt on the funeral pyre of her dead husband. Religious scriptures are misinterpreted by fundamentalist. Even the barbarous tradition of slavery was supposed to have Biblical sanction. It is sheer courage of Mehta that despite all around protests by Hindu fundamentalist, she has brought the in humane practice of widowhood to the surface.

Unlike a novelist, the filmmaker has different tools to express his or her ideas. In a novel, a story teller is generally identified as either first person or an omniscient narrator.In case of film the point of view is told by the camera position and sometimes voice-over narration too is employed.Emotional and intellectual response to a particular moving image is of paramount importance. Often the camera presents an omniscient point of view. Characters are defined, judged, analyzed through their appearances, dialogues and actions which are in fact an outcome of camera.

Watching of Film *Water*: A Visual Literacy

To understand the visual composition of the narrative, the focus needs to be on the techniques while creating the moving images. Clary W.Carleton says that watching films is like getting visual literacy. Being a multi-sensory technology, film is endowed with innumerable meticulously crafted visual and auditory details which need to be read by viewers. *Water*, the film is a very powerful cinematic narrative which takes into account the women struggling against age old rotten cultural tradition in India. Divulging about widowhood Clareton writes:

> Though, the story is set in pre-independence era, most of it is true in even today's society. Nothing has changed for all the good Gandhi's idealism or Raja Ram's sincere efforts. May it be in the social ostracization faced by women on the economic hurdles heaped on them, they are given step motherly treatment? Caustic remarks for the divorced or unmarried women are still in our society. (scribbleofsoul. com)

Though the film is set in 1930s, yet the ill-treatment of widows is still prevalent in India. These outdated traditions exist not only in India but in every part of the world. It is an issue of urgent global concern. In fact, these cultural traditions are used as socio-political tools by patriarchal society to subjugate women. Like the film *Water*, the film *Finzan* (1989) by Cheick Oumar Sissoko, a Malian director and *The Circle* (2000) an Iranian, film by Jafar Panahi are such examples exposing the politics of religion. These two films like *Water* bring forward the female protagonists who challenge traditional cultural practices. '*Finzan*' exposes the glaring sexual inequality which exists in a rural African village where customs refuse to change. Another film worth mentioning is *The Circle* by Jafar Panahi. It is set in modern day Tehran. Reviewing the film, Frederic and Ann Brussat say that the film *The Circle* is riveting Iranian drama set in modern day Tehran, showing how a group of women, severely constraint by the patriarchy, religion, and custom, nevertheless nurture their souls with tonic of freedom. The film depicts the inner yearning of women for freedom. The film fascinates as well as horrifies the audience with its bold assertion about what it meant to be a woman under cruel institutionalized patriarchy. The film opens to the sound of a woman's screams over a black screen. The narrative of the *Circle* begins in a hospital maternity ward, where the unseen woman has just given birth to a baby girl. It will be her ruin, because her husband and in-laws are expecting a boy. This is the end of her brief story, but her name will be mysteriously heard once again at film's end, in a police station.

Women's exploitation is prevalent throughout the world, as Stephan Holden asserts: 'The women work side by side in the fields with their husbands but share few of the men's rights and privileges. When a young woman marries, she becomes a piece of property that can be 'inherited' by male relative when her husband dies" (New York Times 9 December). Similarly commenting about the film *Water*, Burton writes:

> There are thirty four million widows in India according to 2001 census. Many continue to live in conditions of social, economic and cultural deprivation as prescribed 2000 years ago by the sacred texts of Manu, the ancient Hindu Law book. The difficulties of many widows continue despite the Hindu reforms vision of better future. Water is a continuation of this Hindu tradition which, since the 19th century, has sought the social upliftment of the widows by, for example, allowing them to remarry. The promise of reform is presented through the image of Chuyia's potentially happier future; this is what could occur if widows of Indian society changed in accordance of Gandhi's teachings. (1-24)

Reading of the Novel *Water*

Water the novel by Bapsi Sidhwa is an uncommon work because novels are usually metamorphosed into films but films being transformed into a novel is certainly an unusual and a rarer practice. Film makers are inspired by books especially novels and the great classic Hollywood films are inspired by novels. But Bapsi Sidhwa's *Water* is a unique work. Sidhwa did a commendable job as a novelist to write a novel based on a film. Translating a film into a novel is rendering audio-visual experience into words; reversing the common trend of turning novels into films. Here the book adapts film, and the source material is provided by Deepa Mehta's screenplay. Sidhwa's writing of the novel *Water* is an important task. Commenting about Sidhwa's writing a novel based on a film, Assam Ghana states that Sidhwa's idea to write a novel based on a film was an attempt to depict the awareness about the various difficulties these outcaste women face in real life. In writing *Water*, Sidhwa has a created a world she had already imagined while reading the script of the film. She did not lose time to create a back-story for the main character Chuyia, played in the movie by Sri Lankan child actress, Sarla. In this regard Sidhwa herself says, "So, I made this child's background, in doing that I possessed the book. I wrote the book before the movie actually starts. In doing that, I was able to get a handle on this book, possess this child's character, so that I could continue with her and she becomes my character" (moneyvontrol.com). Commenting on Sidhwa's *Water* Sunil Patil concurs: "Bapsi Sidhwa raises her voice against archaic Hindu Laws like child marriage, the caste system, the barbaric acts of Sati, the problems of young widows who spend their rest of time in Indian ashrams to make compensation for the sins in their previous lives"(2).

Both Mehta and Sidhwa have done a commendable job in creating a film and a book. Both of them are an interesting artistic duo. Sidhwa's writing of novel might be to reinforce the idea propounded by Deepa by putting her weight as a serious novelist to a serious issue about the travesties of widows who are forced to live in ashrams away from society. However, reading a novel who has not watched a film experiences a derivative feel. To transcribe the scenes from a film into the pages is a huge task as it is doubly away from reality. It is a well crafted novel which lends beauty to the film from where it is sourced and not the other way round. The book certainly enhances the visual appeal of the film.

Sidhwa's Reasons to Write the Novel *Water*

It is interesting to uncover what would have made Sidhwa write a novel based on a film? Some reasons for the same can be inferred as follows:

- It may be to show her seriousness about the issue undertaken in the film. Both Mehta and Sidhwa are avid supporters of women's rights especially in the Indian sub-continent.

- Novelization helps to elaborate and extend the histories of various characters while the film fails to do so because of time constraint. All the missing links are filled by Sidhwa in her novel. Sidhwa wrote 25 pages to illustrate Chuyia's family background. An elaborate description is made about the village she lives in. Her playing with dolls, searching some ripe gooseberries and finding Tun-Tun, the puppy in distress etc. The novel also gives us detail about her brothers, Prasad and Mohan. Characters of Madhumati and Gulabi are also described in some detail.
- Novelization makes the film coherent. Novel that is the mode of an excess unlike that of a film is copious whereas film isn't. Novel makes the film clearer from where it has been novelized. Film *Water* runs too fast to be comprehended by the Western audiences who are alien to the concept of widowhood. In the film within five minutes we see Chuyia is seen to be forsaken by her father and mother-in-law at the vidhwa-ashram with shorn head. The meaning of breaking her bangles, snapping of her *mangalsutra,* shaving of her head, forcing her to wear white clothes sometimes may not be understood by the audience in the Western world. Sidhwa's novelized version makes it quite clear to the readers about the entire concept of widowhood and makes the film coherent.
- To convey what was unsaid. Generally it is a novel that gives birth to a film but sometimes film gives birth to a new form of fiction.But the important question is what is the need to write a novel based on a film? What made a writer of Sidhwa's stature to write a novel based on a film? Sidhwa is a novelist of enormous talent. She is capable

enough to create her own story line. The most suitable answer to this question is that she wanted to give an elaborate description to the ideas of Mehta. She wanted to say what she thought remained unsaid.

- Cinematographer's use of camera angle (high, low, overhead) to create a particular effect revealing shifting point of view. Since a novel is voluminous and is not subjected to time limits, Sidhwa wrote *Water* the novel based on the film of the same name. The Film is more coherent than a novel. Novel is copious whereas film isn't. Sometimes the reader may be bored by excessive descriptions in the novel.
- Another aspect of novelization is that it makes the film clearer. Novel makes the film clearer from where it has been novelized.

Water the Film versus *Water* the Novel

Both the film and novel are two different entities. Both have advantages and disadvantages associated with them. These are discussed as follow:

Economic Implication

Writing a novel being inspired from a film involves lesser economic implications. Film on the other hand is purely subjected to its commercial aspect. It is subjected to the laws of market. Film production is based on the principal of economic viability. As far film *Water* is concerned; the economic implications are far more significant because the film was stopped in India by Hindu fundamentalist. The early financer Ajay Virmani dropped the project. But Mehta is a woman of iron resolve. Canadian Tele Film Limited financed Mehta to make the film. It involves sale of tickets, contract of music and other market features. Film is like a mirror.It is created by the device called camera. To hire best quality camera, equipments, actors and set building etc., a huge investment is required. Novel on the other hand is not influenced much by the laws of economics. Selling of few thousand copies make a substantial profit. Novel is created through a pen which is not an expensive device.

Use of Colours in the Film *Water*

Colours are used to create or manipulate a particular atmosphere or mood. Film *Water* is replete with colours which are used extensively especially blue and white. The film provides a spectacle of colours. Both these colours raise the issue of purity. Widows in the ashram are forced to wear white clothes perpetually which makes the colour look oppressive. All the widows are draped in white including Kalyani who looks stunningly beautiful in whites. This is a religious instruction to remain in a state of chastity out of respect for their dead husbands. This concept of purity is designed hypocritically to keep widows subservient. Not only widows but other characters like Narayan are also dressed in white, describing him Sidhwa writes: "He wore a sparkling white dhoti with long, graceful pleats in front and a white shirt" (Water 61).

There is also ample display of blue colour. Blue is the color of our planet since the seventy percent of the earth is water. The use of deep blue colour plays a larger motif of water as a place of ritual cleansing, death and rebirth. In India white colour traditionally symbolizes mourning and purity. Water is an elixir endowed to give and take life. In Hindu tradition water symbolizes feelings, intuition and imagination which interestingly are associated with femininity. This is absolutely appropriate because the film is about women. However, the colour blue is also used in the film *Water*to symbolize the challenge of dogmatic representation of purity, self denial and obedience. As the film begins, a bullock cart is shown passing on the fringe of a large pool overgrown with lotus. And the first focus is on the wheels which have spokes having blue colour. The yoke of the bullock-cart is also coloured blue. The Ganga River looks like a blue sheet. And then we see Chuyia wearing a blue sari. Colours play an important role in the film *Water* symbolizing purity and annihilation.

Element of Sound and Song in the Film *Water*

Besides colour, sound and songs also play a vital role in the film. The eminent film critic Christian Metz has written that a film is difficult to explain because it is very easy to understand it.Films are being watched by spectators uncritically, sitting in the dark. Films have three important components by which it is created: visual, aural and linguistic. Introduction of songs and music accentuate these elements. A thorough analysis of these components is of vital importance to read films. Keeping in mind the Indian audience, Deepa Mehta introduced song sequences in her film *Water*. The song sequences in the film are: *1. Bhangari... marori... 2. Nainaneer... 3. Piya ho...4. Sham rang de rang de ... 5. Vaishnavajanato...*

The first song is sung by Sadhna Sargam and Sukhwinder Singh and is 5.17 minutes long. The Music is given by A.R.Rehman. The song is: *Bhangari marori meri saiya ne meri,*The second song sequence in the film *Water* is: "*Chhan chhan chhanan chhanan chhanchhan, Gunjegi aaj murli ki dhun.*" Another song sequence is: *Naina Neer, Naina naina neer bahaye, Naina naina neer bahaye.* This song is written by Sukhwinder Singh and is sung by SadhnaSargam. The fourth song sequence is: *Piya ho pia ho... Chali main chali main piya, Lekar preet ki reet, Sang sang chale mera aas ka gagar...*And the last and most important song sequence is Gandiji's favourite hymn:*Vashnava janato tene* *kahiye, Je Peed parai Jane re, Je peed parai Jane re, Vaishnava janato tene kahiye.* This song is sung by Kaushki Chakrabarty and Ajoy Chakrabarty and music is given Narsinh Mehta.

Water the Film versus *Water* the Novel: An Analysis

Despite having faced many hurdles in making the film *Water,* Mehta made a wonderful film. The screen play is very crisp and well knit. Shrugging aside all the difficulties and controversies, Mehta made a movie which was a commercial success. "*Water,* the movie has already made waves as it proved a commercial success in Canada and has gathered critical acclaim in the U.S." (moneycontrol.com). Undaunting Mehta, created ghats on the bank of Sri Lankan river made a film ready to shake the Hindu fundamentalist.The movie is bold and unapologetic for being so. It shows the truth as it is. "Water is so real and passionate that you will easily be moved and shacked" (data/data/com.android.com).

The film is focused on the main theme and does not divert at all. The dialogues in the film are amazing. The Chyuyia-Kalyani, Chuyia-Shakuntala, Kalyani-Narayan conversation is superbly crafted and cinematographed. Music in the film seems to blend into scenes beautifully. Sarla, representing Chuyia is faultless. She is perhaps the best actress in the film. She is cute, energetic and a perfect choice for the role of Chuyia. She looks convincing but fails to capture the heart and soul of the spectators. While watching the film one loses the emotional grip because of the Lisa Ray's average acting in the film. She seems more refined than is needed in the film especially in the later part of the movie. John Abraham in the role of Narayan, the Gandhian has not done the justice to his role. Seema Biswas in the role of Shakuntala is simply outstanding. She is a perfect choice of Mehta and she has done justice to her role. Even the original choice for Shakuntala

(Shabana Azmi) may not have done the kind of justice to the role that Seema Biswas has. She received Film Fare Lux Genei Award for best performance by an actress in a leading role for the film *Water.* Manorama in the role of Madhumati is also amazing. She has been able to create a sense of awe and fear in the ashram. She is perfectly vile as the plot demands. Raghuvir Yadhav is a heartless eunuch.Kulbhushan Kharbanda in the role of Sadanad is commendable. But reading a novel after watching the film is certainly more absorbing. Expressing her views about the film *Water*, Jannette Catasouls describes that the film *Water* is an exquisite film. It brings institutionalized oppression of an entire class of women by patriarchal forces to the surface. Serene on the surface yet rolling underneath; the film neatly parallels the plight of widows under Hindu fundamentalism. The movie is never didactic, trusting the simple rhythm of women's lives to tell their story.

No doubt the movie was marvelously made but reading of the novel is more absorbing. Sometimes one has to struggle to experience the emotional touch in the film *Water* whereas the stream of emotions flow free in the novel. Despite being an adaptation of the screen play the novel seems to capture the essence of story more profoundly and extensively.

CHAPTER-III

Feminist Reading of Literary Texts–*Water, Earth* and Film Texts–*Earth, Water*

> In [Deepa] Mehta's oeuvre, transnational realities are deftly acknowledged and straddled alongside a feminist ethical stance. (Sharon Tay Lin.119)

Bapsi Sidhwa and Deepa Mehta had made a genuine contribution to the feminist narrative, former through fiction and latter through films. Both of them are known for their social concerns especially about the women of the Indian sub-continent. Divulging about the gender inequalities in all societies, Amna Khalid writes:

> Gender inequality and exploitation has been prevailing in all societies of the world since the ancient times and it is still there in the era of enlightenment and awareness about the equality of rights among male and female sex. Majority of the societies in the world are male dominated and women are treated just as an object for pleasure there, not as esteemed creation of God. They are not given equal rights as to the men and they are mostly exploited by the men existing in their surroundings. (amnakhalidraja.blogspot.com)

She believes that the male dominated society always tries to manipulate the laws and rules to overpower and subjugate women. New unjust laws are being created by patriarchal societies to silence woman. This chapter gives an insight into the selected texts under the scanner of feminism. An elaborate and extensive investigation is made about the issue of feminism from the Stone Age itself. During the Stone Age, spade and hoe were the only implements used by humans. These implements established woman's strength for gardening. They gathered nuts, seeds and wild plants. There seem to be some equality between the two genders. Mentioning Engels' views in his *The Origin of the Family, Private Property, and the State,* Simone de Beauvoir says that when man hunted woman used to remain at home to take on the task of domesticity which included productive labour-making pottery, weaving and gardening. Hence woman played a large part in economic life.

Anthropologists believe that with the dawn of agriculture, people started accumulating resources for the first time and with this an imbalance emerged. And men started having several wives and had more children than women. Anthropologist, Mark Dyble says that it pays more for men to start accumulating resources and becomes favorable to form alliances with male kin. Also with more technological changes such as the advent of copper, tin and iron, woman's fate took a turn. The scope of agriculture increased and man started clearing woodlands for more cultivation. More labour required. In this regard, Simone de Beauvoir writes:

> Then man has recourse to the labour of other men, whom he reduces to slavery. Private property appears; master of slaves and of earth, man becomes proprietor also of woman. This was the great defeat of feminine sex. (85)

A woman who had occupied a good position in the Stone Age

seems to give way to man. Maternal authority diminished and paternal authority started ruling the roost. Now property was inherited from father to son and no longer from woman to her kith and kins. A woman was confined to domestic duties. Man became everything while woman was reduced to a trivial entity. As a young girl she is under the control of her father, when she marries she comes under the control of her husband. She became like a property to different men in patriarchal societies. But in matrilineal societies, despite many taboos, women do possess some freedom, and chastity is rarely required. Since then all vices are perpetrated on women in the name of religion. However, with the passage of time, efforts were made to establish equality between the two sexes which slowly but surely led to the advent of ideology of feminism.

Feminism is broad and complex ideology having variegated meanings. It is a term frequently used in everyday life. Though there is not a single definition that could define feminism completely. Some of them are: "Feminism is a doctrine advocating social, political, and all other rights of women equal to those of men" (dictionary.com). Defining feminism, Mitchell A.states that it is an initiated struggle of women in creating solidarity with each other, against the norms and values of male dominated world and their sexist policies. Feminism aims to question the concept of male-chauvinism. It is targeted at male patriarchy which has been playing havoc on the lives of women from the centuries. Talking about feminism Rengin Ozan writes:

> The term feminism describes the utopia view of the equality between men and women in equal terms of what both gender are able / expected to do, in terms of personal characteristics, actions and lifestyles. Feminism allows women to step outside their culturally created gender roles and perhaps take on a job or activity or lifestyle that is not traditionally

> female, and thus allows for the freedom of choice, which is what we think feminism is at the core, the power of choice and individuality free from gender norms and cultural expectations. (Rengin Ozan. 84)

However, the most common and understandable meaning is described by Roger Scruton who describes it as a movement advocating the rights of women and of their social, political and economic equality with men. Gender equality, gender roles, gender stratification, women's welfare, sexual justice are some common ideals. All varieties of feminism contain at the core a common goal of requiring gender consciousness. As a movement, feminism vehemently opposes the gender stratification in all its forms. Feminism promotes social, political, economic and sexual equality for men and women. Most feminists believe that men and women should not be judged on the basis of sex. They should be judged who they are as an individual. Feminists strive to fill the chasm that divides men and women. To understand feminism some attention is given to understand the concept of feminine principle. In this regards Ranchan and Razdan state, "The feminine principle manifests itself as sex, as womanhood, as devotion, and surrender to the masculine and finally as that which makes us accept life as life, without reference to the shadow world of ideas" (47).

It is imperative to throw some light about the different waves of feminisms.

First-Wave Feminism

'First-Wave feminism' refers to the period of feminist activity during 19th and 20th century throughout the world, particularly in the United Kingdom, Canada, the Netherlands and the United Sates.It focused on women's suffrage i.e. the right to vote. Mirriam Schneir talking about the first woman who "takes up her pen in defense of her sex" was Christine de Pizan in the 15th century.Mary Wollstonecraft in her treatise, *A Vindication of Rights of Women* (1792), advocated social and moral equality of the sexes and she is regarded as the grandmother of British Feminism.

Second -Wave Feminism

'Second-Wave Feminism'started in early 1960s and lasted 1980s. It raises the issue of women's social and sexual concerns. Second wave feminist voiced to uncover the patriarchal influences not only politically, socially but also about their sexual existence. They challenged the prevailing notions of the women's role in the family, work place and society. They criticized the sexual division of labour and voiced for promoting the women's equality in labour market. They addressed the issues like equal pay, employment and educational opportunities, reproductive rights of women. Women's well being was the priority. Divulging about gender equality Lena Dominelli Mcleod asserts: "We are equal irrespective of our gender. Social relations that obliterate this fact must therefore be transformed and recreated in ways that reflect equality in terms of gender" (1).Kate Millet in her book *Sexual Politics* defined the 'patriarchal government', as an institution in which one half of the population controls the other half. Then radical feminism is a concept which holds the view that gender equality can be established only by eradicating the cultural notion of the gender. This view holds the opinion that patriarchal forces perpetrate women subordination through sexuality and reproduction. Men give vent to their masculine prowess through women's' bodies. It is through their bodies; men celebrate victories, moan defeats and take revenges. Feminists want to develop human choices as they maintain that the cultural perception of gender, divides the full range of human qualities into two opposing and limited spheres: the female world of emotion and cooperation and the male world of rationality and competition. As an alternative, feminists want to pursue a 'reintegration of humanity'by which each person develops all human traits regardless of whether they are male or female.

Third-Wave Feminism

'Third-Wave Feminsim' identifies several aspects of feminist activities. It started with realizing the fact that second-wave feminism has failed to address and incorporate the voices of young, queer and non-white women. It was the movement of women of many colours, ethnicities, nationalities, religion and cultural backgrounds. It is clear that the history of women from times immemorial has been restrained by innumerable principles and prejudices cultivated by patriarchal society, mechanism of patriarchy, the cultural mind set of men promulgated sexual inequality. This inequality between the sexes exists from the prehistoric times, except the Stone Age, and is established by the research related to ethnography.Simone de Beauvoir writes:

> I have already stated that when two human categories are together, each aspires to impose its sovereignty upon the other. If both are able to resist this imposition, there is created between them a reciprocal relation, sometimes in enmity, sometimes in amity, always in a state of tension. (93)

It is therefore understood that man would wish to dominate woman; but it needs to be questioned what advantage has enabled him to carry out his will? Woman's existence is severely limited in the patriarchal world. The woman has been pinned down to her domestic chores all her life. She is forced to stick to her household duties. In the patriarchal world, the women are eulogized for petty things.

In the present chapter an emphasis is made to explore the four texts in the feminist perspective. A male dominated society has been stifling women's capacity to be independent in thought and action. Bapsi Sidhwa in her novels and Deepa Mehta in her films have exposed the patriarchal society. Women in both the novel as well as in the film, take the mechanism of patriarchy head on. Since the proposed texts deal with women of the sub-continent, it is imperative to have an insight about the status of women in the Indian scenario.

Women's Status in Ancient India

Raja Ram Mohan Rao, the great social activist was known as the first male feminist for his efforts to abolish Sati. Describing woman he writes:

> Woman is earth, air, ether, sound; woman is the microcosm of the mind, the articulation of space, the knowledge, the woman is fire, movement, clear and rapid as mountain stream; the woman is that which seeks against that which is sought. To Mitra she is Sita, to Krishna she is Radha. Woman is the meaning of the word, the breadth, touch, act...and indeed even when the king is crowned it is the queen to whom the kingdom comes. (352-53)

In order to understand the feminist perspective in the proposed texts, a need is felt to acquaint with the status of women in ancient Indian society. Most scholars are of the view that the women held an elevated position in ancient India. During Vedic period, women held similar position as men possessed. Women who were inclined to religion wore sacred thread and also were taught mantras of the Vedas. Women of Kshtriya caste got martial art training. They were very skillful in arms training. Writing about ancient women, Niramal Laungani says that the Vedas, Upnishads and other scriptures give numerous examples of women philosophers, politicians, teachers, administrators and saints. The Rig Veda says that the wife and husband are equal halves of one substance; they are equal in every respect; therefore both should join and take equal part in all works, religious and secular. The Ancient Hindu scriptures enshrined great regard for women. Girls are respected as the forms of goddess Lakshmi. But the status of women declined during epic period. In Ramanaya, two incidents, Sita's *Agni Pariksha* and her banishment to the forest do throw some light on the subjugation of women. In this connection, Afreen Faiyas writes:

> Feminism is an extension of existentialism, finds an echo in world literature. The existential struggle to establish one's own identity, to assert ones individuality and the desperate fight to exist a sseparate entity appears in all intensity in the novels of women writers of the Indian subcontinent , like Anita Desai, Shashi Deshpande, Rama Mehta,Chitra Bannerjee, Nayantara Sehgal, Taslima Nasreen and Bapsi Sidhwa. (pakistanpaindabad.blogspot.com)

Women in the Manu Samhita

But Manu Samhita, written long after Vedic periods is replete with derogatory statements about women. Film *Water* by Deepa Mehta begins with epithet from Manusamriti. The film *Water* as well as the novel of the same name deal with the issue of widowhood in the times of 1930s India. The 2000 years old sacred texts by Manu, the Hindu progenitor of mankind writes that a virtuous wife is one who after the death of her husband constantly remain chaste and had to lead a life of an extreme depravity. As Sara Barrera describes that widows in India have a pronoun problem. The estimated 40 million women widows in the country go from being called "she" to "it" when they lose their husbands. They become "de-sexed" creature. But the problem of widowhood is not confined to India only, it has universal proportion. Commenting about Mehta's concern for widows and worldwide problem of widows, Manju Jaidka writes:

> The problems Mehta focuses on are not limited to the Indian soil. One may cite the Loomba Foundation which presented the first edition of the study, *Invisible Forgotten Sufferers: The Plight of Widows around the World*' to UN Secretary General Ban Ki-Moon, in New York as a part of its campaign. The report says the countries with the highest number of widows in 2010 were in China with 43 million, India with 42.4 million, the US with 13.6 million, Indonesia with 9.4 million, Japan 7.4 million, Russia 7.1 million and Brazil 5.6 million. The plight of these widows, the study tells us is pathetic. When their husbands die some women are required to be 'cleansed', some are erroneously accused of murder or witchcraft, some are required to marry another member of the family, many are disinherited and forced out of their homes and many are raped. Foundation reports that around 115 million widows live in poverty across the world. (69)

Everywhere in the world different methods are used by patriarchal society to subjugate women. The issue Deepa Mehta and Bapsi Sidhwa have addressed has a universal significance. This chapter focuses about the plight of Indian widows of 1930s of Pre-Independent India when several restrictions were imposed on widows.They were enforced to shun colorful clothes, eschew their jewellery and even shave their heads. This was all done not to arouse male sexual desire. This is an ugly and atrocious way of draining the essential elements of femininity out of them. Certain restrictions are imposed on their diets too. Onions, garlic, pickles, potatoes and fish which are supposed to arouse sexual desires by stimulating the blood are put out of their meager diets. And they become the victims of malnutrition. Hence both in the film as well as novel, all the elderly widows are depicted mere skeletons.

The novel *Ice-Candy-Man* and in the film *Earth*, addressed the issue sexual politics. All the women characters seem to assert their individuality. Ayah, Godmother, Lenny in the novel *Ice-Candy-Man* and Kalyani, Shakuntala and Chuyiain the novel *Water*, do struggle to establish their individuality against the backdrop of male dominion. Even Madhumati, the caretaker of the ashram was once the victim of patriarchy.

The women characters in the novel *Ice-Candy-Man* refuse to sacrifice everything at the altar of patriarchy. They challenge the patriarchal mode where the men control everything. Men seem to salute women's beauty but not their emotions. Women are treated partially in the Indian society. Women had been receiving a partial treatment ever since patriarchal forces have been at play. Man has become the subjugator and woman the subjugated. It is not linear, nor is it a well organized structure. The civilizations from the very beginning had been very partial in treating women. Feminists sought to fill the chasm between man and women created from centuries by patriarchal prejudices.

Many biological handicaps such as pregnancy, childbirth, and menstruation reduced their capacity for work and they became at times wholly dependent upon the men for protection and food. Once they became dependent upon men, their subjugation at the hands of men started. Commenting further, Simone says that the existentialist perspective has enabled us to understand how the biological and economic condition of the primitive horde must have led to male supremacy. Girls are told from their infancy how to behave and act. In this regard Mary Wollstonecraft, an advocate of women's rights says:

> Women are told from their infancy, and taught by the examples of their mothers, that a little knowledge of human weakness, justly termed cunning, softness of temper, outward obedience, and a scrupulous attention to a puerile kind of propriety, will obtain for them the protection of men; and should they be beautiful, everything else is needless, for at least twenty years of their lives. (28-29)

Similar views are expressed by Neera Desai and Usha Thakkar. As they assert:

> The good woman is sweet, gentle, loving, caring and ever sacrificing. The main stream concept of the role of woman sees to best described in the anonymous Sanskrit couplet: She (in relation to her husband) is like mother while cooking and serving food, secretary while he is working, servant at his feet, courtesan in his bed and earth – like in forbearance. (1)

The women are forced to conduct themselves in a particular way ever since from their infancy.They are advised and even enforced to act in certain way just to earn men's praise and protection. Explaining the plight of woman, Simone de Beauvoir opines:

> One is not born, but rather becomes a woman.No biological, psychological, or economic fate determines the figure that the human female presents in the society; it is civilization as a whole that produces the creature, intermediate between male and eunuch, which is described as feminine. (295)

At every step society does not hesitate to demean woman. They have to struggle against the apparent disadvantages of the female body. Simone further says that the very concept of 'woman' is a male concept. The woman is always 'other' because the male is the 'seer': he is the subject and she the object – the meaning of what it is to be a woman is given by men. A woman was defined from male point of view. Attention was given to books by male writers in which typical images of women were constructed. But from 1970s some attention was given to women writings and slowly it gained momentum. As Peter Barry writes that it was Elaine Showalter who described the change in the late 1970s as a shift of attention from 'androtexts' (books by men) to 'gynotexts' (books by women). Commenting about her he writes: "She coined the term 'gynocritics', meaning the study of gynotexts, but gynocriticism is a broad and varied field, and any generalizations about it should be treated with caution" (Peter Barry 118).

It was Showalter who first detected the history of women's writings in a *feminine phase* (1840-80), in which women writers imitated dominant male artists, their norms and aesthetic standards; then a *feminist phase* (1880-1920), in which radical and often separatist positions are maintained; and finally a female phase (1920 onwards) which looked particularly at female writing and female experience. All the four selected texts taken under study are all 'gynotexts.'

Ice-Candy-Man and the *Earth*: A Feminist Perspective

Ice-Candy-Man as well as well *Earth*, the film version of it deals with the theme of partition. In both these texts it is the woman who performs and controls the action. Both Sidhwa and Mehta, raise women's issues to the forefront. The issues such as violence perpetrated on women during partition in various blatant forms are brought to the surface in *Ice-Candy-Man* by Sidhwa as well in its cinematic adaptation the *Earth* by Mehta. Talking about partition and the consequent migration, William Dalrymple writes that in August, 1947, when after three hundred years in India, the British finally left, the subcontinent was partitioned into two independent nation states: Hindu majority India and Muslim majority Pakistan. Immediately , there began one of the greatest migrations in human history, as millions of Muslims trekked to West and East Pakistan (the latter now known as Bangladesh) while millions of Hindus and Sikhs headed in opposite direction. Many hundred thousand never made it.

Both novel as well as the film depict the picture of partition of Western Pakistan. The communities who have been living in harmony for almost a millennium attacked each other. Hindus and Sikhs on one side and the Muslims on the other carried out a mutual genocide. The worst victim was a woman. "Nisid Hajari, in "Midnight's Furriers" (Houghton Mifflin Harcourt), his fast pace new narrative history of Partition and its aftermath, writes, 'Gangs of killers set whole villages aflame, hacking to death men and children and the aged while carrying off young women to be raped. Some British soldiers and journalists claimed Partition's brutalities were worse: pregnant women had their breasts cut off and babies hacked out of their bellies; infants were found literally roasted on spits." (Before its News)

Ayah (Shanta)both in the novel as well as in the film, represents those ill fated 83000 women (55000 Muslim, 33000 Hindus and Sikh women) who were abducted, raped and were kept as forced wives during partition. Thousands were killed by the people of faith other than theirs. Thousands were killed by their own fathers, brothers and their relatives in the name of honour. Revenge of all sorts was inflicted on women's body irrespective of religion. In the name of honour women were sacrificed. Describing one such incident Urvashi Butalia writes:

> In one of these villages, Thoa Khalsa, some 90 women threw themselves into the well in order to preserve the 'sanctity' and 'purity' of their religion, as otherwise they would have had to

> face conversion... the tales of women's sacrifice occupy an important place... It is they who are seen to have upheld, by offering themselves up for death, more particularly 'heroic death,' the 'honour of the community. (12-24)

Women as the Victims

Women of all religion became the victims of false male chauvinism.The women characters in the novel, be it Ayah, Lenny or Godmother, all exhibit an extraordinary courage, resilience and individuality not to be easily subjugated. It is their sheer valour that they exposed the patriarchal prejudices rampant in the contemporary society. Sitting on the fence, Sidhwa gives an authentic account of partition in its flagrant nakedness and brutality. However, she gives the Pakstani perspective a little edge. But her delineation of women characters is beyond borders and territories. Her characterization of women characters is different from the traditional one. Commenting about Sidhwa's women protagonists Subhash Chandra writes: "Bapsi Sidhwa turns the female protagonists into the moral centre, while most of male characters either remain apathetic or indulge in destructive violence and disintegrating actions" (Chandra 177).

All of them represent endurance; their capacity to fight and survive. They personify the extra-ordinary resilience of women in the times of utmost difficulty. Inter-racial harmony of pre-independence is cracked in backdrop of partition. The threads that bound the society for centuries were snapped by the jolts of partition. The society which lived in harmony was torn and divided on racial, religious and political lines triggering a mass slaughter. The selected texts such as *Ice-Candy-Man* and *Water* are feminist texts. The former brings to the surface the wounds inflicted on women during partition. It deals not only with the assaults inflicted on women of the subcontinent but also divulges the utmost valour the women displayed in the most difficult times. It offers a very important aspect of feminine psyche. Sidhwa explicates the gynocentric view of reality through her various women characters such as Ayah, Lenny, Mother and Godmother. These four women protagonists exhibit an extraordinary resilience in the wake of utmost brutality being perpetrated by men, especially on Ayah. The patriarchal biases are present in the contemporary society like ugly sores.

Being a Parsee as an impartial observer, Sidhwa brought to the surface the mayhem perpetrated by Hindus, Sikhs and Muslims. She did not belong to either of the two communities. She presented this drama of partition impartially. She gives us a very objective and neutral account of the traumatic event of the partition which broke the century old ties of mutual harmony and caused divisiveness, suspicion, hatred and hostility between the two communities. Women became the victims on both sides of the border. Sidhwa depicts the events in their candid cruelty and callousness. It is very courageous on her part of Sidhwa to take on the issue of women which is unconventional. It's truly a feminist text. Sidhwa brings her women protagonists to the kernel of morality. Most of the male characters such as Ice Candy Man, Masseur, and Butcher remain indulged in destructive violence. They appear to indulge in verbal violence before going into physical one. While her female characters throb with life of their own despite being the victims of phony male morality. Sidhwa's women characters cut loose the social constraints imposed on them. The century old patriarchal social constructs are deconstructed by her. She disapproves the notion that patriarchy is associated with masculinity, superiority and strength whereas femininity is linked with weakness, inferiority, submission, passivity, timidity, self-sacrifice, self-negation and blind obedience.

In the name of culture all types of sanctions are imposed on women. In this regard Tania Bansal states that the violence upon women is perpetrated in almost all sections of society.In the name of tradition and culture women are exploited everywhere. Rape is one such act. Talking about rape which is used as a device to subjugate woman, Jayant Rana writes: "Rape is about silencing a human being, that silencing continues inside a 'normal' household too where a man with all his privileges can decide whether to report a crime or not while a woman keeps her silence even when she disagrees" (38). Women are the victims of violence irrespective of class and religion. Clark, C. Fiona and Caroline O.N. Monser mention the plight of woman in the following lines:

> I am a woman
> I want to raise my voice
> Because Communalism affects me
> In every communal riot
> My sisters are raped
> My children are killed
> My men are targeted
> My world is destroyed
> And then
> I am left to pick up the pieces
> To make a new life
> It matters little if I am a Muslim, Hindu or Sikh
> And yet, I cannot help my sisters
> For fear that I may be killed or
> That they may beharmed. (Zubaan)

But Sidhwa's novel, subtly but effectively challenges the deep-rooted elements of patriarchy. Her women character exhibit extraordinary forbearance along with the feminine qualities of kindness, empathy and motherhood. She displays different colours of feminisms in her novel '*Ice-Candy-Man*. How women characters are portrayed during the times of utmost adversity are discussed as follow:

Lenny: The Girl Child Narrator

Lenny is the child narrator. She was born in a Parsee family. Sidhwa delineates the central consciousness of her world. It is a bold attempt on the part of Sidhwa to give a girl, a status of narrator. Sidhwa has done a commendable job in bringing forward the social, religious and political upheavals of the time through the eyes of small polio struck girl named, Lenny, a young Parsi girl growing up in Lahore. Commenting about the girl child narrator Lenny, Subhash Chardra opines:

> The lameness of the narrator-protagonist becomes suggestive of the handicap a woman creative writer faces, when she decides to wield a pen, because writing, being an intellectual exercise, is considered a male bastion, outside the routine of woman's submissive domesticity. Her recuperation symbolizes the overcoming of the constraint on the intellectual activity of writing by Bapsi Sidhwa. By making Lenny the narrator of the novel, the novelist lends weight and validity to the feminine perspective on the nature of surrounding reality. (177)

She narrates the story of partition of India amid the domestic atmosphere of her family and friends around. Novi Kapadia explains that Lenny can be compared to the persona that Chaucer adopts in his Prologue to *The Canterbury Tales*, rendering credibility by being almost a part of the reader's consciousness. It is through Lenny's observations that we came across all social, cultural, and political changes that took place in Lahore during partition.

Lenny's Sexual maturation: A Bold Characterization

But the most important aspect of feminism is depicted through Lenny's sexual maturation. The novel is a story of eight-year-old girl Lenny turning into a young woman and her maturation and sexual awareness. It is an audacious attempt on the part of Sidhwa to depict the process of sexual maturation of a young girl Lenny in the country like Pakistan. Commenting about Lenny's sexual maturation, Subhash Chandra writes: "It is no mean achievement on Sidhwa's part to depict the process of sexual maturation of a young girl while living in the country like Pakistan where the measure of freedom for women is considerably less than it exists in India." (Chandra 176). It reminds us of Maggi Tulliver as is viewed in the Observer 'The novel is about the slow awakening of the child heroine both to sexually and grown-up pains and pleasures to the particular historical disaster that overwhelms her world... compulsively readable. Lenny reminds of Maggie Tulliver.' Writing is considered as an intellectual exercise beyond the women's means. They are restricted to domesticity. But Sidhwa's writing symbolizes the overcoming of the impediments being imposed on women.

By making Lenny as the narrator of the novel, the writer puts her weight and validity to the feminine perspective. *Ice-Candy-Man* being a feminist text involves actions centering round women protagonists. There are women who acquire the attributes of heroism and grandeur, unlike that of male discourse in which women remain the beneficiaries of male bounty and bravery. Throughout the novel, Lenny does not allow her cousin (cousin in the novel without any identity of a male) to manipulate her sexually even though he keeps doting on her. She maintains her superiority over him, though at times he seems to be aggressive.

But Lenny's lameness in no way hinders her in asserting her. In no way does Lenny's lameness become a source of self-pity or constricting force on her psyche. She remains assertive, at times even aggressive and holds her own when it comes to the crunch. She is also quick learner as Sidhwa writes:

> I learn fast... I learn of human needs, frailties, cruelties and joys... I have many teachers. My cousin shows me things... He has just returned from Quetta where he had a hernia operation. 'Let me show you my scar,' he offers, unbuttoning his fly and exposing me glamorous spectacle of stitched scar and handful of genitals. (ICM 20)

The novel very boldly delineates her sexual maturity. It's a step forward on the part a girl child towards sexual maturation because she is becoming smart enough to know about the clever fingers of cousin like that of Ice-candy-man. In delineating Lenny's character, Sidhwas's gynocentric views of reality are displayed with freshness and bloom. She brings her female protagonists to the center as in Jane Austen's Mansfield Park, Fanny Price the female protagonist who had been marginalized is brought to the moral center. In most of the partition novels such as Khushwant Singh's *Train to Pakistan* (1956), most of the male characters are involved in violence and disintegrating actions and women characters are merely the victims. But Sidhwa's women characters exhibit extraordinary courage even after brutally assaulted in their body and mind.

Revelation of Feminine Qualities

The novel *Ice-Candy-Man* resonates with feminine qualities of forgiveness, resilience, compassion and motherhood. Describing about Lenny's learning and growth, Jahanzeb Jahan asserts:

> As a young girl she sits in Queen's garden with her Ayah, her nanny, who is nubile and the object of desire for large circle of young men of many races and creeds. Young Lenny perceives their eyes burning for Ayah, their furtive attempts to touch her with their hands, mouths and even their toes. Her education about sexuality begins early though Sidhwa delights in showing us Lenny's later sexual discoveries as well, such as growing aware of her cousin's body. (slideshare.net)

Lenny's constant vigil *at Ice-Candy-Man's* toes comes as lesson in growth towards sexual maturity. In her own words it is said:

> Sometimes a toe snakes out and zeroes in on its target with such lightening speed that I hear of the attack only from Ayah's startled Oaf!' Once in while I pre-empt the big toes' romantic impulse and, and catching it mid crawl or mid-strike, twist it. It is measure to keep the candy bribe coming. (ICM 19)

Lenny's extracting candy bribes even from the person like Ice-Candy-Man is certainly her stepping forward towards maturity. It's a story about baby-Lenny and her coming of age during the time of partition. The story corrodes the veneer of peace and tranquility and exposes the deep rooted prejudices created by religion, race, colour, class and income inequalities to the surface. The novel brings political short-sightedness in its most naked and brutal form. It portrays the life of ordinary people caught in the whirlpool of extraordinary times. It tells the story of partition of India through the eyes of nine year old Parsee girl, Lenny. Like Sidhwa, her narrator Lenny is a child born into an upper class Parsi family. She is a privileged child. Sidhwa presented the partition with double impartiality, by virtue of Lenny, her narrator a child and without any ethno-religious affiliation.

Deepa Mehta, on the other hand, was born into a Hindu family in Amritsar and her family migrated to Canada during partition. The idea of the inclusion of biographic elements is to suggest that the politics of ethnicity plays an important role in understanding both the texts: novel and the film. Sidhwa presents a neutral position the Parsi community took during partition. As Col. Bharucha says: 'We must hunt with the hounds and run with the hare' (ICM 16). Lenny, a precocious child describes the brutality of partition with chilling veracity. Like the author, Lenny is stricken with polio and is extremely observant narrator though at times her understanding is limited by her childlike innocence. According to Jahanzeb Jahan, "Bapsi Sidhwa delicately threads the story of an 8 year old girl named Lenny with the din of violence ready to crash around her world as the partition moves from political planning to reality. The story is told in the present tense as the events unfold before the young girls' eyes" (slideshare.net).

Ayah: An Epitome of Female Resilience

Ayah (Shanta) is perhaps the most influential character in the novel as well as in the film. She is the major female voices in both the novel as well as in the film. *Ice-Candy-Man* is essentially her story. It is the story of her world surrounded by men belonging to different social as well religious strata. Like a magnet she always attracts different males like iron flints as they come in the radius of her charm.She is like flame of sensuousness and female *joie de vivre* around whom the male moths linger constantly and long for the sexual warmth she emanates.

Commenting about her magnetic attraction, Subhash Chandra says, "She is like a queen bee that controls the actions of her male admirers. But this all happened during the times of peace and harmony. Her admirers are: the Government House Gardner, the Falletis Hotel Cook, the Butcher, the Masseur, and the Ice-Candy-Man" (178). Her influence over them extends to such a measure that they readily decide to stop the political discussions for her sake. Ayah has tremendous impact on Lenny, another female protagonist. She infuses the idea of independence and about making choices in Lenny. She has the strongest influence on Lenny. Ayah knows herself well, and she is confident enough as an individual, who cannot be taken advantage of. Ayah is the formative influence on Lenny. "Epitomizing the strength of feminity of a female, she infuses in Lenny the idea of independence and choice. Flirtatious and coquettish, the Ayah is fully aware and confidant of herself as an individual, who cannot be taken advantage" (Chandra 178). Besides, she is an embodiment of loyalty to the family she serves. She is always keen and observant and is extremely protective of Lenny. She is emotionally attached towards Lenny like a mother. The texts, film as well as the novel display her faithfulness and devotion to the family she serves. She suffers but remains loyal to the family till she was dragged out, ravished and raped by hooligans. The film ends with her abduction. Whereas the novel, *Ice-Candy-Man* explains what happens to Ayah after her abduction.

> She suffers during the partition riot; she is abducted by the cronies of the Ice-Candy-Man, ravished and raped by the hood looms, kept as Ice-Candy-Man's mistress for few months and then is forced to become the Ice-Candy-Man's bride. Her name is changed from Shanta to Mumtaz and she is kept at a *kotha* even after marriage. During the interregnum between her abduction and marriage, she, in the words of Godmother, is "used like a sewer" by "drunks, peddlers, sahibs and cut throats," with connivance of the Ice-candy-man. (Chandra 178)

She was forced to live as Ice-candy-man's mistress for few months and then forced to become his wife. During this period from her abduction to marriage she was used as an object. But she would not yield to her tormentor and when opportunity came, she escaped from the clutches of the man she does not love. She firmly says that she wanted to go to her family. She is in no mood to forgive her tormentor.

Lenny's Mother: Traditional Image of Womanhood

Lenny's Mother, another woman character who sticks to traditional image of womanhood. She conforms to the conventionally established symbol of femininity. She represents the conventional view of fidelity, faithfulness and servitude which are attributed to women as their finest qualities. She yields to the whims and fancies of the man she is married to. She tolerates male superiority. Sidhwa presented her as the woman adapted to live in her domestic habitat. But remaining rooted to her home; she displayed an extraordinary courage to save Ayah. She exhibited an exceptional humanitarian outlook even though she and her family members were in extreme danger. When Lenny accuses her in augmenting the communal conflagration by smuggling the rationed petrol, she says: "We were only smuggling the rationed petrol to help our Hindu and Sikh friends to run away..... And also for the convoys to send kidnapped women, like your Ayah, to their families across the border" (ICM 242).Here we see the courage and grit of this woman to help the people who do not belong to her community. She displays the most beautiful feminine quality of compassion, helpfulness and courage.

Godmother (Rodabai): An Embodiment of Courage, Confidence and Authority

Godmother (Rodabai) is another important character in the novel who plays a vital role in the novel to represent true feminine spirit. She stands high among these women protagonists. Though, the film does not have this character, but in the novel her vibrant personality dazzles with wit, courage and stamina. She has unbound love for Lenny. She is devoted to social commitments. She has great capacity to handle situations. She is glorious example of self confidence and authoritativeness. She is very tough in dealing *Ice-Candy-Man.* She has a wonderful sense of humour. She has a great sense of wisdom too. She is an influential figure in the novel. She is a vivacious woman brimming with courage, sharp wit and wisdom. She has a profound understanding of human nature.The territory of her influence radiates all around. As Sidhwa writes:

> "Nobody-not even kitten-is delivered within the spheres of her influence without her becoming instantly aware of its existence. And this is the source of her immense power: this reservoir of random knowledge, and her knowledge of ancient lore and wisdom and herbal remedy. You cannot be near her without feeling her uncanny strength. People bring her to their joys and woes. Show her their sores and swollen joints."And "she has access to many ears". (ICM 211)

The manner in which she consoles Ayah reveals her wisdom. When Ayah says that she cannot forget what has happened to her, Godmother comforts her and says: "That was fated, daughter. It can't be undone. But it can be forgiven...Worse things are forgiven. Life goes on and the business of living buries the debris of our pasts. Hurt, happiness...all fade impartially... to make way to fresh joy and new sorrow. That is the way of life" (ICM 262). Her advice to Ayah is like a spring of cool water. Her words soothe Ayah and she feels somewhat comfortable. She is in fact the most effervescent example of self confidence, authoritativeness and astuteness. She has an incredible capacity to handle situations. The manner in which she handles and admonishes Ice candy man after Ayah was kidnapped and kept at a *kotha* is simply compelling and potent. Ice-candy-man, a man gifted with a glib of a tongue, is not an easy person to deal with. But Godmother is fully equipped to overpower her opponents.Her apathetic silence makes Ice-candy- man edgy and he lowers his eyes, such is her indifference. He was unnerved and says:

> 'I am her slave, Baijee. I worship her. She can come to no harms with me.'"No harm?" Godmother asks in a deceptively cool voice-and arching her back like a scorpion its tail, she closes in for a kill. 'You permit her to be raped by butchers, drunks, and goondas and say she has come to no harm?'.Ice-candy-man's head jolts back as if it's been struck. Is that why you had her lifted off- let hundreds of eyes probe her-so that you could marry her? You would have your own mother carried off if it suited you! You are a shameless badmash! Nimakharam! Faithless! (ICM 248)

Such is the sway of Godmother's power. She visits the disreputable "Hira Mandi" (the area of *kothas*) and rescues Ayah. Once she is convinced that the Ayah is being kept by force against her will, she wastes no time to liberate her. This deed is commendable. Godmother possesses all those traits in her character which are important for a woman to realize her individuality-the feeling of "self-worth". Summing up her character Subhash Chandra concurs:

> Towering high among the women protagonists is the vibrant

> figure of Lenny's Godmother (one of her aunts) whose name is Rodabai) Godmother's personality sparkles with razor-sharp wit, her indefatigable stamina, her boundless love for Lenny, and her social sentiment. Her sense of humour, her deer-like agility, in spite of her old age, and her power to mould, modify and order not only individuals but even the system, when she so desires, earn her respect and admiration of people around her.(179)

She is an embodiment self-confidence, courage and authority. She possesses an unbound power to annihilate her adversary.

Ayah's resilience in the face of utmost difficulty, her firm rejection of Ice-candy-man despite her weaknesses, Godmother's ingenuity, and her strong resentment for *Ice-candy-man* show the women's prowess. And above all, the process of recovery-all combine together to make this novel a great 'gynotext'. It is endowed with women centered stories. This is a novel in which women are pitted against patriarchal set up during the chaotic times of partition. The women are not willing to give up; they are ready to take reins in their own hands, particularly Ayah, after being intrigued, abducted, and raped. She is not willing to yield.

However, the film ends with Ayah's abduction. Not only in *Ice-Candy-Man* but in her other novels such as *American Brat*, Sidhwa explains the various kinds of marginalization. Her women characters are treated as sexed subalterns. But they are all the force to reckon with. *Earth* film ends with the abduction of Ayah by the crazy crowd led by the man who once loved her. Describing the brutal treatment meted out to women during partition David Lester, a renowned British-American psychologist and suicidologist writes:

> In particular, the humiliation of women was foremost, including raping and disfiguring women in front of their

> relatives, tattooing and branding them with 'Pakistan, Zindabad' or 'Hindustan, Zindabad' marking ahalf-moonon their breasts and genitalia, and amputating their breasts. (Suicidology-online.com)

Not only during partition but ever since the advent of civilization, history seems to have been silent about women. Stating about untold troubles women suffered during partition Ritu Menon and Kamala Bahasin observe:

What did independence mean to women who suffered its most violent consequences? What was the nation to them? Homeland?Religion?Freedom itself? Where did they find their place in this land of redrawn boundaries? Widows from 1947 are still to be found in ashrams and permanent liability homes in Karnal. Delhi, Rohtak, Jullandhar, Amritsar... It is from them and scores of others that we heard about much that has remained hidden from history. (24)

Four years after Independence more than 30000 thousand women were recovered. How they were recovered is another story, no less painful.

Godmother–Slavesister Relationship

The novel *Ice-Candy-Man* also exposes another kind of filial relationship. We come across constant rebuking of Slavesister by Godmother. She is treated poorly by her own sister Rodabai. She is scolded frequently in presence of others. She is always suppressed and is not allowed to exercise her own views in any situation. Though this relationship seems to serve no purpose in the novel as far as plot is concerned, this part is not an indispensable part of the story. But, Sidhwa has taken into account an issue of women exploitation, oppression of one individual by another in the home itself. She wanted to bring to the surface the suppression of women by women. Through this Godmother-Slave sister relationship, Sidhwa wants to bring to the fore the intensity of this type of exploitation being perpetrated by women on women. Sidhwa wants to illustrate this issue impartially. By highlighting this type of the relationship, Sidhwa has presented herself as an impartial delineator and makes her feminist perspective wider, fairer and more accountable. In a true sense, the novel *'Ice-Candy-Man,'* successfully brings the female protagonists to the core. Besides being individuals, they facilitate to raise feminist consciousness among women. Sidhwa belongs to that rare group of women for whom the traditional and conventional roles were inadequate. They are the women who assert their independence. They are the women capable of assuming any responsibilities.

Feminist Reading of the Film *Water* and the Novel *Water*

Water, the film as well the novel deal with the issue of widowhood in pre-independent India of 1930s and take on the issue of feminism in both the texts. Mehta's film *Water* and its novelized version *Water* by Bapsi Sidhwa reveal the important issue of widowhood. In ancient India an extreme solution to widowhood was to burn the wife of deceased on the funeral pyre of her dead husband. Both the film as well as novel bring forth predicament of widows in pre-independent India of 1930s and the awful condition they are forced to live in. Mehta and Sidhwa, the former with visual images and the latter with words expose the distortion of religion by fundamentalists for their own personal gains. As David F. Burton states:

> Water is set in sacred Hindu city of Varanasi in the 1930s and examines the plight of a community of socially ostracized widows.Their lives are governed by many social and

> behavioral restrictions such as taboos against remarriage and physical contact with high-caste Hindus. (2)

The film *Water* by Mehta begins with an epigram on the blank screen. "Widow should be long suffering until death, self-restrained and chaste. A virtuous wife who remains chaste when her husband dies goes to heaven.A woman who is undutiful to her husband is reborn in the womb of jackal." The Laws of Manu Chapter 5 verse (156-161) Dharamashastra (Sacred Hindu Text). Inequality and degradation of women is almost sanctified in Hindu religion. Manu Samriti says:

> Never trust a woman. Never sit alone with a woman even if it may be your mother, she may tempt you. Do not sit alone with your daughter she may tempt you. Do not sit alone with your sister, she may tempt you. And same Samriti continues, "*Na stree swadantriya marhathi.*" "No liberty for women in society." Women are never fit for independence. (Manuscript 9: 2-4)

Widows were treated as *Kulachani* (an evil omen), an economic burden. They have to live bare foot, sleep on the floor and are not allowed to venture out of the house. All sorts of restrictions are imposed on widows, which have universal dimensions. And this type of exploitation exists not only in India but throughout the world. This type of exploitation is also exercised in other societies throughout the worlds. Writing about Nigerian society; Mary Imelda Obianuju Nowogu states that women are regarded as their husband's property or chattels. They are compelled by cultural practices to be and remain subservient to their husbands. The subservient nature of women during their husbands' life time is carried into the death their husbands thereafter. The widows are forced to go through an excruciating mourning observance. The hair of her head and body are compulsorily shaved. The widows are excluded from the ownership of landed property. They are forced to observe many rituals such as mourning rituals and food taboos that are enforced on widows all over the world. They are pushed into economic hardships everywhere in the name of culture. In the name of tradition, the rights of widows are grossly refuted. The schemes employed to ill-treat widows are almost similar everywhere. They are forced into seclusion. Grief ridden widows lose the will power to challenge these practices and their perpetrators. In this scenario, the marriage of widows was out of question during ancient times. But this is disgusting, especially to modern women. Mehta and Sidhwa took it on stride to hit hard at this age old rotten tradition. Mehta made a film portraying the time of 1930s of India when Gandhi's influence was visible everywhere. Kalyani-Narayan relation, in the film as well as in the novel both throw some light on the gravity of widow's re-marriage. Mehta's film *Water* focuses on a very important issue concerning women. It deals with the problem of widows in India in the year 1938. This was the time when men were the champions of society and women were not allowed to make their own decisions. In this regard, Amita Nijhawan writes:

> A film is about anguish of widows in 1930s India, where widowhood was in many parts of the country taken to be the curse, an affliction that the widow paid penance for by living in renunciation of laughter, and pleasure, Water points out not only the suffering of widows in colonial India but the widow-house that still exists in Varanasi and the homes for poor widows in seclusion and disgrace, away from the community. (journal. media-culture.org.au)

The widow-homes are still full to their capacities in the city of Varanasi. Girls were married off in very tender age to older men through arranged marriages. As in the film *Water*, Chuyia a girl of eight is given off in marriage to HiraLal, a man of forty four years. Mehta portrays the plight of child widow Chuyia. Undoubtedly, she strikes hard at the existing patriarchy.

As the film opens, Chuyia is accompanying her dying husband, unaware about her future. He dies and she becomes a widow. Her head shaved, bangles broken and is brought to widow ashram at Vrindavan. Her father tells her, Chuyia, "Child. Do you remember getting married? Your husband is dead. You are a widow now" (Water 32).Chuyia becomes widow at the tender age of eight when she doesn't understand the meaning of marriage. Divulging about the novel, Afreen Faiyas writes:

> The novel located in 1938, nine years before India freed itself from the shackles of colonialism, is based on the treatment of Hindu widows in traditional societies. *Water* does not have any Parsi, Muslim, Sikh or Christian characters, but focuses on Hindu characters. The novel completes the circle, encompassing all communities, in depicting injustice towards women that is not limited to a particular sect, caste or society but is universal. After Zaitoon, Carol and Ayah, the Hindu widows in India that highlighted are hapless slaves to ancient traditions and superstitions. (ox for dbibliographies. com)

Afreen rightly describes of the plight of Hindu widows. The patriarchal forces are always in a ready state to grab an opportunity to exploit widows for their personal gains. But all is done in the name of religion. When Som NathChuyia's father asks her:

> Bitiya, do you remember getting married?" The question was of no great importance to the child, and Chuyia shook her head from side to side. 'No,' she said in a clear voice. 'Your

> husband is dead,' 'You are a widow now'. Chuyia was untroubled by her father's pronouncement, having no concept of the impact of those words on her life. (Water 32-33)

Sidhwa describes the events in detail. As in the very first chapter of the novel, Somnath, Chuyia's father tells his wife Bhagya that HiraLal's mother wants Chuyia to marry HiraLal, her son. Bhagya is shocked to know this. Somnath says that he has already agreed."I have agreed,' he said. "Their horoscope matches. I have looked at some auspicious dates. They want the marriage to take place before Diwali-in September or October. The monsoon will be over and guest can sleep outside" (Water 6 -7). Even a man like Somnath who is otherwise meek and submissive, takes it as his male privilege to take a decision of his daughter's marriage without even consulting his wife. For him the convenience of guests during marriage is more important than the life of Chuyia who is merely eight years old. And her prospective husband HiraLal is of forty four years old and is a grandfather. Shocked Bhagya says, "shouldn't you have consulted me?" (Water 7). His reply is "How could I refuse HiraLal's mother?"(Water 7). In the fit of rage she says, "It is settled then! Why bother to tell me? So what if I have never set eyes on the man?"(Water7). And only wish she could utter "Eeshh, Bhagwan: may she never come of age!"(Water 7). Such is the helplessness of a woman. Pacifying her, Somnath tells her that after all girl is destined to leave her parents. The earlier it is the better it is. She says, 'She is safe and happy only in her husband's care.' 'In the Brahminical tradition,' said Somnath, 'a woman is recognized as a person when she is with her husband. Only then does she become a *sumangli,* an auspicious woman, a *saubhagayavati,* a fortunate woman' (Water 8). He too regards woman as a commodity to be handed over to the man, well in time. The statement he makes that woman is recognized as a person only when she is with her husband. So he is in a hurry to marry off his daughter and regards a girl the burden who carries the seeds of dishonor until she was married . Somnath is shocked to hear Bhagya who says staring at him, 'And you think that man will be able to satisfy her *stri-svavahava*? By the time her woman hood blooms, he'll be old and spent' (Water 8). Somnath is stunned to hear this from his wife. To talk about women's sexuality is like a sin. In this regard Manju Jaidka writes:

> If we consider examples from the past, we note that in the Indian tradition, sexual desire is a subject best kept out of the public eye. Ironically, in the land which produced Kamasutra, sexuality belongs to the private sphere and is not discussed in public. As for female desire, it is even more taboo in India-in fact, it is considered to be nonexistent. (20)

Talking about sexual cravings and innate sexual desire of women, Uma Chakravarti writes: "There [was considered] no greater delight and no more destructive urge for women than sex" (63-69).

A woman is a goddess beyond sexual craving but if gripped by passion she is nothing short of monster. Bhagya's talking about woman's innate '*strisvabhava*' especially of her daughter's, perturbs Somnath. Though he cherished his wife's passionate nature but to hear her speak about her daughter's sexuality stunned him. He does not want to hear all this. His ideas of sanctity, based on Brahminical tradition, were shattered to pieces. Defending this age old tradition, he says, "Brahmin elders were right: women were dangerous" (Water 8).

The patriarchal society from ancient time had been in a habit of throwing blame on women. When the wedding took place in the village temple, all the villagers, guests and relatives were served *kheer* in shallow earthenware dishes in the temple it self while the menstruating women were left food at the temple doors lest their presence defile the wedding as well as temple. This is another social restriction employed by patriarchal forces to segregate women. Almost all the major religion of the world Juadaism, Islam, Hinduism and Buddhism placed restriction on the menstruating women. All sorts of prohibitions are imposed on menstruating women. The idea to impose certain restrictions during menstruation is given in the Manusamriti, a text written by Manu (who is man).And all texts written by men are prejudiced and flawed. There is no such restriction written in the Vedas (Yajur Veda, Rig Veda, Atharva Veda, and the Sama Veda). It is not even written in the Gita, Purana or Mahabharata. When Draupadi was disrobed by the Kaurbas, she was menstruating. We all know Lord Krishna himself rescued her.God only wants pure devotion. The idea to put restriction on women is again an offshoot of evil minded patriarchal mind set. Later Chuyia's mother Bhagya does not forget to remind her that she is married and she must take care to cover her head. She warns her not to jump and romp around. When Hira Lal succumbed to fever and dies young Chuyia becomes widow. Describing the plight of widows, Sidhwa writes:

> She knew that in Brahmin culture, once widowed, a woman was deprived of her useful function in society- that reproducing and fulfilling her duties to her husband. She ceased to exist as person; she was no longer either daughter or daughter-in-law. There was no place for her in the society. (Water 24)

She ceases to be even human and is reduced to be a mere object. Elaborating further Sidhwa writes: A woman's sexuality and fertility, which was so valuable in his lifetime, was converted upon his death into a potential danger to morality of the community

(Water 24). This exposes the double standard of Hindu society.

Chuyia's Passage into Widowhood: A Tormenting Episode

After the death of HiraLal, Chuyia's father declares that her husband is dead and she has become a widow. The child innocently asks him for how long, realizing not the concept and widowhood at that time. Her dead husband's body is hoisted on the wooden funeral pyre for final rite.Sidhwa describes the incident:

> His body was wrapped in a white cloth, but his face was exposed. With child's curiosity, she studied her dead husband. His eyes were closed, and lit by the fires his face appeared to have acquired a ruddy glow; in a sudden flash of memory Chuyia saw him decked out as groom, and thought, that was my wedding day. (Water 32)

Later Chuiya's mother-in-law did not waste time to jerk the *mangalsutra* off her neck and the beads scattered on the ground. Little Chuyia is shaken. She seized Chuyia's hand and violently smashed the red glass bangles with a piece of brick.

Then, methodically, with no more concern for the girl than if she were an inanimate object, she took the other hand and with the brick smashed the bangles on her other wrist. Chuyia, struck speechless, looked at her shattered bangles in dismay... Chuyia realized with a stab of shock that she had ceased to matter to this woman. (Water 33)

Chuyia could make out that she is now an inanimate object to her mother-in-law. After smashing her bangles, other women pulled down Chuyia's skirt and pulled her blouse up over her neck and saying, "You can't wear colours or stitched clothes,' threw them in a heap to one side" (Water 33). We see women too are not lagging behind in exploiting women. And then finally the little widow is led to one of the ghat's barber for shaving of her head. Describing the incident Sidhwa writes:

> There was genuine sadness on his face as he examined child's hair to decide how best to proceed. He had never tonsured such a young widow before. Chuyia turned her large somber eyes on him, and he smiled at her kindly, and then firmly turned her face forward. As he snipped off the first of her long tresses, the barber initiated the next ritual in Chuyia's passage into widowhood. (Water 34)

Chuyia's father Somnath sees this tormenting ritual with agonizing pain and watched all this with utmost sorrow while HiraLal's mother blames the howling child for a karmic debt of past sins that had deprived her of her son. Chuyia was forced to live with other widows, Shakuntala, Patirajji, Kalyani, Kunti and many others, wrapped in white clothes with shaven heads except Kalyani. Chuyia's mother-in-law blames Chuyia the innocent child of eight years for being the reason of her son's death. This is contemptible, unbelievable and weird.

Kalyani (Lisa Ray): A Victim of Religious Hypocrisy

Kalyani, another important woman character both in the film as well as in the novel is an embodiment of womanhood. She is exploited by the people who are always there masked in as the well-wishers of the society. They distort religion to their petty interests. It is the economic vulnerability which forces Kalyani into prostitution. As Malini Bhattacharya states: "Kalyani, who has been forced into prostitution, a fate which has not been unusual for economically vulnerable women in Widows ashram" (81).She is stunningly beautiful young widow with long black traces. She was probably nineteen or twenty years old. Sidhwa describes her: "Her eyes, wide beneath the thick arches of her brows, were friendly and kind. They were the shape of color of almonds. To Chuyia, she seemed like an angel" (Water 51). She is the bread winner for the ashram. To look attractive her head is not shaved. She is forced into prostitution to support the ashram. Talking about widespread prostitution in different ashrams in India, Doctor Hitoshi says that the flesh trade flourishes in Vrindavan and Mathura in the full knowledge of the police, administration, holy men, and politicians. Kalyani is the victim of the lust of rich land lords, so called philanthropists who are willing to pay for their lust and make the ashram run.In this regard Amita Nijha wan writes: "The film opens the lens to the prostitution and privation experienced by many widows, as well as Gandhi's efforts to change the laws that affected "widow-remarriage" (journal.media-culture.org). She is caught in the whirlpool of Hindu society as the women characters are caught in the vortex of Muslim society in Tehmina Durrani's *My Feudal Lord* and *Blasphemy.* TehminaDurani another Pakistani author like Bapsi Sidhwa is an ardent believer in women's rights.Her sensational literary debut novel '*Blasphemy*' is a searing study of evil. It depicts how Islam is distorted by the predatory religious leaders. Pir Sain, the so called man of God, brutalizes Heer. All in the name of Allah; unspeakable horrors are perpetrated every day and night. Pir Sain, a monster in the garb of religion inflicts all types of physical as well as mental pain to Heer. Describing one such incident Durrani says, "Gripping my arm he pulled me into the courtyard and pushed me down. He kicked I stood up. He pushed until I fell. Pushed and kicked, I reached the kitchen door" (47).

Both Mehta and Sidhwa expose the distortion of religion in Hindu society. People miss no opportunity to disgrace the widows. Chasing 'Kaalu' the dog, Kalyani trying to catch it up slammed into a stout, colorfully attired woman returning from the river. Admonishing she yells:

> "You have no shame." Grabbing Kalyani by the arm she said, "You have no morals! You are a widow, and yet you run around like you are an unmarried girl?" Then she yanked her arm away as if she'd been stung and hissed, "You've polluted me. I have to bathe again!" (Water 59-60)

Kalyani lowered her head pulled the *pallu* of her *sari* to the tip of her nose thought like burrowing into the Earth.

Narayan's Decision to Marry Kalyani

Waiting for Chuyia who was chasing Kaalu the puppy, Kalyani happens to meet Narayan, a Gandhian. As Kalyani was reprimanding Chuyia, Narayan saw her. He was enthralled to see her as Sidhwa writes: "He stood transfixed, completely enchanted, and stared at her as if she were the first woman created by God.Their eyes met… Narayan was struck mute, mesmerized by the contours of Kalyani's perfect face, which at that moment was being licked enthusiastically by Kaalu" (Water 63-64). Narayan falls in love with Kalyani, tells his mother about his decision to marry a widow. His mother is shocked and can't believe him. But Narayan like a true Gandhian is determined to marry Kalyani. He takes her home. Describing this short home journey Sidhwa writes:

> As the boat took a bend in the river, a bulky white mansion, with turrets and bulging towers and haphazardly tacked on extensions that reflected different architectural eras, rose like an ungainly galleon from bed of rock and trees at some distance behind Kalyani.'Look-that's my house,' Narayan said, gesturing towards mansion. (Water 170)

She was flabbergasted and shaken to see the house. She stood frozen. The colour was drained from her blushing face, she turned pale."An ominous chill coursed through her blood and drained the colour from her face. Kalyani turned her eyes to Narayan and in deathly quiet voice she asked, "What is your father's name?"'Dwarkanath...Seth Dwarkanath.' The blood chilled to ice in Kalyani's veins and turned her body numb" (Sidhwa 171). Seth Dwarakanath, Narayan's father has been using Kalyani for his sexual gratification. As Kalyani comes to know about Narayan being the son of Dwarakanath, she is taken aback. She ordered the boatman to turn around immediately. Unbound dread crept across her face and she stood up making the boat bobble perilously. Firstly, Narayan could not make it what his father had to do with Kalayani's resolve to turn back. Describing Narayan's understanding of her determination to turn back Sidhwa writes, "As a glimmer of comprehension dawned at the edges of his mind, he was overcome by a deep foreboding. Histhroatconstricted and then swelled" (Water172).

DwarkaNath, Narayan's father is an embodiment of shamelessness. He thinks what has happened is unfortunate. It has nothing to do with morality.

'I'm sorry you are disillusioned, son,' he said, speaking kindly and with as much dignity he could muster under the circumstances. 'But you cannot go through life being so idealistic.' Turning his palms out to indicate that the situation was not as serious as Narayan believed it was, he said, 'So you've found out she is not a goddess. Don't marry her-keep her as your mistress. (Sidhwa Water 173)

Such is the shamelessness of Dwaraka Nath. He has no regrets. He lacks the morality which he thinks has nothing to do with what he has been doing with Kalyani. Look at the shamelessness of a man who boasts to be the exponent of

Hinduism. For Narayan, the Gandhian, it is unbelievable. Looking at his father in disbelief when he came to know about his father' (Dwaraka Nath's) real self. But Dwaraka Nath is unfazed; he placed a placating hand on Narayan's shoulder and says:

> "Narayan, perhaps you are not aware of this. Our holy texts say Brahmin can sleep with whomever they want, and the women they sleep with are blessed."...Such is the hypocrisy of Brahmins...Narayan stood flabbergasted at the shamelessness of his father... 'I have studied our scriptures,' he said, breathing heavily and struggling to retain some control over his voice. 'God Ram told his brother never to honour those Brahmins who interpret the holy texts for their own benefit'. (Water 174)

After returning, Kalyani has no place to go. She sits on the gravel outside Madhumati's room. Madhumati had warned her not to come back to the ashram. Her dreams to marry Narayan are shattered. Several questions came to her mind."How could she have ever imagined she would marry Narayan? Had she seduced him with languishing looks, small flirtations? Would he still want to marry her now that he'd more time to mull over the matter? What contempt and loathing, would the Seth have for her? What must his mother think of her? This was unbearable" (Water 175-176).What if she is not given shelter in the ashram? She had two options. First to cast out in streets and die there. And to return to the life of forced prostitution without Narayan. Without Narayan to die is a better option than to live. Kalyani leaves the ashram dragging her to the ghats. She stepped into the waters of the Ganga.

The cool water seeped through her sari, but her body was so cold that it felt warm against her skin. She removed a brown cloth-band from her wrist, and set it gently on the top of the folded sari. Kalyani rose and walked slowly into the river until the water came up to her knees. She went to splash her face with the sacred water that flowed from Shiva's head, and smeared it over her face and hair. She clasped her hands in prayer for a moment. Then she calmly walked into the river until her short hair floated in an inky stain on the water."Ma Ganga had claimed her daughter." (Water 177- 178)

This is how Kalyani dies, a victim of putrid patriarchal thought. She wanted to grow like a lotus untouched by the dirty water it grows in. The age old cruel shackles of chauvinistic patriarchal thought choke her to death. She represents thousands of such widows who are still leading a life of hell in various ashrams.

Shakuntala: A Widow Torn Between Religious Faith and Human Desires

Shakuntala (Seema Biswas) is middle-aged widow, living in the ashram. She is enigmatic, considerate and devout Hindu widow dwelling there. She is torn between her religious faith and human desires. She takes on Madhumati, the head widow to save Chuyia as well as Kalyani. She defies Madhumai and frees Kalyani to have her desires fulfilled. She is a mother figure to Chuyia. When Kalyani could no longer satisfy the ravenous lust of rich Brahmin Seths, Chuyia is tricked by Gulabi in connivance with Madhumati to take her place. When Shakuntala comes to know about Chuyia's absence in the Ashram, she runs frantically to find her out like a tigress searching for her lost cub. She rushes into the widow's room and in the kitchen. A stab of fear shivers through her and races into Madhumat's room. "Shakuntala shook Madhumati's shoulders and demanded, 'Where's Chuyia?Have you seen Chuyia?' Her voice was hoarse with fear" (Water 187).When Madhumati does not respond she shakes her harder and her teeth rattled and her voice cracking with anger. "Madhumati opened her drugged eyes with difficulty. They were bloodshot, and the pupils were dilated. 'I've sent her.' Her speech is slurred, and the words dribbling from her mouth end on a note of finality that Shakuntala's hear" (Water 188). She slaps Madhumati and flees from the room with clenched fist. She rushes out of the ashram, into the dark gullies and reaches at the ghats. Finding for boatman, all were done for the day. She is desperate. When she spots Gulabi, she shouts at her. And "Like a mother bear whose cub is endangered, she was quite liable to bound into the boat and thrashes the life out of her. Before the boat could come to a stop, Gulabi leaped onto the embankment and, grunting in fear, fled flat-footed past Shakuntala"(Water 189). Chuyia was lying in the boat. She had been drugged. Shakuntala tries to wake her up and pleads her to open her eyes. She takes Chuyia in her arms.Takes her to the river washes her face. She is dazed with horror to see the congealed blood from cuts and wounds. It is Shakuntala, who made Chuyia revive.

It is Shakuntala who makes a plan to save Chuyia and ensures her rescue to board Gandhi's train. As the train arrives, she pleaded desperately to take the child. "Listen to me... Why don't you listen? Why don't you understand? Sisters! Please take her with you! Please listen! This child is a widow" (Water 197). As the train starts speeding, a hand reaches out from the train towards her and Chuyia. Narayan is leaning precariously from the train holding on with one hand, extending the other to grasp Chuyia and holds Chuyia up in his arms. Running with the speeding train Shakuntala pleads, 'Make sure she's in Gandhiji's care.' 'Yes, Didi,' he replied. Commenting about Shakuntala's effort to save Chuyia, Panini Wijesirwardena and Parwini Zora assert:

Moved by Gandhi's brief comment that the pursuit of truth should be one's religion, the distressed Shakuntala pleads with various people to help her save the child widow by "giving her to Gandhi". The film concludes with Shakuntala discovering that

Narayan has decided to join Gandhi's journey. He takes the child as the train departs the station. (wsws.org)

It is apparent that it is Shakuntala only who consoles Narayan when Kalyani commits suicide. When Narayan came to take her, he was too late. He stood against a brick wall, unable to take his eyes away from Kalyani's pyre. Shakuntala tries to console Narayan and says, "The holy texts tell us that all this is Maya, an illusion."…"Kalyani's death is no illusion", Narayan said, the peremptory tone and his gruff voice expressing some of the anger within him (Water 180). She moved closer to him. "Narayan, no matter what happens, you must not lose faith,' she said, laying her hand on his shoulder" (Water 180).Shakuntala is an embodiment of womanhood having her faith rock solid even in the times of extreme adversity. She did not lose faith and is determined to hand over Chuyia to safety. She acts like Chuyia's surrogate mother. After handing over Chuyia to Narayan, Shakuntala watched the train carrying her till it vanished into the dark green trees in the distance. Shakumtala plays a very pivotal role in saving the child Chuyia. She is portrayed both in the film as well as in the novel with equal profundity. Deepa and Sidhwa's women are rock solid. Reviewing the film, Frederic and Mary Ann Brussatremark:

> *Water* the film asserting that it depicts the terrible danger can be done to the human spirit when chauvinistic religion rules and texts are treated as sacrosanct. The inhumane treatment of widows in India by Hindu fundamentalist is similar to subjugation of women by fundamentalist Christian, Jews and Muslim elsewhere. It is appalling to see religion used to deny the dignity and rights of women. Deepa Mehta has done all women an immense service by making this extraordinary film about the liberation their sisters yearn for with their hearts, minds, bodies and souls. (spritualpractice.com)

Talking about her film *Water*, Mehta states that water can flow or water can be stagnant. The film is set in the 1930s but the people in the film live their lives as it was prescribed by the religious texts more than 2000 years ago. People follow the texts which is one of the reasons why there are millions of widows in India. She wishes that traditions shouldn't be that rigid. They should flow like replenishing kind of water and not like the stagnant water. Mehta is a humanist film maker deeply concerned for society. Amy Fung writes about her "As a humanist film maker [Deepa] Mehta has demonstrated her penchant for creating complex human dramas in equally complex social settings" (80). The film by Deepa Mehta is an extraordinary attempt to depict the plight of widows in India who yearn for liberation of their body and soul. Both Sidhwa and Mehta contributed immensely to feminist issues. Both exposed the society's callous behavior towards women. Both are the champions of women's cause. All their women characters do not lose faith, be it Ayah of *Ice-Candy-Man* or Shakuntala of *Water.* All the four selected texts are truly 'gynocentric texts'. Both hit out at the phony and untruthful morality prevalent in Hindu society.

Chapter-IV

Film Texts–*Earth* and *Water*: Under the Lens of Feminist Film Theory

This chapter focuses to study film texts *Earth* and *Water* under the lens of feminist film theory. In order to understand feminist film theory, first we need is to understand film theory. The Film theory is an academic discipline closely allied with critical theory which aims to find out the essence of the cinema and provide conceptual frameworks for understanding film's relationship to reality, the other arts, spectators and the society at large. It is explained as the study of filmmaking from the technical aspects of making a movie to its relationship to other art forms and its effects on society and culture. This is not an independent field of study. It is associated and borrows ideas from other branches of study. It is an integrated study associated with psychology, philosophy, art theory, linguistics, cultural theory, literary theory, social science, economics and political science.

Film theory has its birth during the period of silent cinema (1895-1929). It is a collection of interpretative frameworks developed over a period of time in order to understand the way films are made and received. Earlier it was focused on defining and understanding the newly invented medium. The film theory evolved slowly but surely being influenced by the works of eminent directors, film critics and film theorists such as Hugo Munsterberg, Rudolf Arnheim, Louis Delluc, Jean Epstein, Sergei Eisenstein, DzigaVertov, Lev Kuleshov Bela Balazs and Siegfried Kracauer etc. Hugo Munsrterberg and Rudolf Arnheim considered silent film to be art because it does not merely mechanically record reality but transforms the normal ways in which the human eye perceives, through editing, camera angles and black and white photography. These concerns were revisited by later theorists such as Christian Metz. Writing about film theorists before 1945, Malcom Turvey, a film scholar says that the film theorists before 1945 used to compare and contrast cinema to other art forms, especially to the theatre to which cinema was seen as bearing the greatest resemblance. These film scholars were the people who emphasized how film is different from reality and how it is a very valid art form. However, after World War II, Andre Bazin, a French film critic sharply reacted against this approach to understand film as different from reality. He argued that the film's essence lay in its ability to reproduce reality, not by an argument that the film is different from reality. But during 1960s and 1970s, film theory broadened its scope by importing and assimilating the already established disciplines like psychoanalysis, gender studies, anthropology, semiotics, linguistics and other literary theories in its fold. During 1990s, the sudden spurt in technology especially the digital revolution has impacted the film theory in number of ways. Film theorists like Laura Mulvey considered psychoanalytical perspective after Lacanian notion of real. Slavoj Zizek gave a new aspect of gaze to be used in film analysis. It has now branched out into several other specializations because of various other approaches to study it. One such approach is to study it under the lens of feminism. This approach gave birth to Feminist film theory.

Feminist Film Theory

Feminist film theory had its origin in the 1960s. But the year 1972 seems to be the watershed year for the feminist film theory. Stating about the development of feminist film theory, RenginOzan writes:

> The feminist film theory was influenced by second wave feminism and the development of women's studies within the academy. Feminist scholars began taking cues from the new theories arising from these movements to analyzing films. Initial attempts in the United States in the early 1970s were generally based on sociological theory and focused on the function of women characters in particular film narratives or genres and of stereotypes as a reflection of societies views of women. (74)

'Women's Cinema As Counter Cinema' by Claire Johnston and the article of Laura Mulvey "Visual Pleasure and narrative Cinema "are considered and widely accepted as the first theoretical studies of feminist cinema. Johnston is of the opinion that feminist cinema may be a counter cinema and may be an alternative discourse against Hollywood films in terms of not only production but content also. Claire Johnston's *Women's Cinema as Counter Cinema* (1973) is perhaps the earliest piece of writing about feminist film theory. She shows how women have been stereotyped in the films ever since the days of silent films. She argues and challenges such a narrow conception dominated by male vision. A woman is merely presented as spectacle. Stating about woman's representation in the films, there are scholars who are of the opinion that despite having an enormous emphasis placed on woman as spectacle in the cinema, they are largely absent. *Popcorn Venus: Women, Movies, and American Dream* (1973) by Marjorie Rosen, *From Reverence to Rape: The Treatment of Women in Movies* (1974) by Molly Heskellare some pioneer works in this regard.

Analysis of films how the women are portrayed in broader historical, sociological and stereotypical depiction are taken into account. Laura Mulvey's influential essay expands it further. It brings to the surface the concept of passive representation of women in the film. She argues about 'male gaze'. In this regard, Annette Kuhn in her book Women's Pictures writes:

> In North America, a number of women's film festivals – the first New York International of Women's Films (1973)-coincided with the publication of the three books of feminist film criticism: Molly Haskell's From *Reverance to Rape* (1975), Marjorie Rosen's *Popcorn Venus* (1973) and Joan Mellen's *Women and their Sexuality in the New Film* (1974). (72)

These were the books with revolutionary ideas about the inclusion of women in the films. In the year 1976, came the first issue of a 'journal of feminism and film theory', *Camera Obscura*. This new journal took up the issue of feminism from structural, cultural, political, economic and psychoanalytical standpoints. But in the past 25 years Feminist Film Theory has become a large and flourishing field of film study.

Different approaches of film studies are exemplified in the journals such as *Screen* and *Camera Obscura*. The dominant approach involves a theoretical combination of semiotics, Althusserian Marxism, and Lacannian psychoanalysis. Added to this theory by Laura Mulveys's now-classic essay, "Visual Pleasure and Narrative Cinema" [Mulvey, 1975], was that the men and women are differentially positioned by cinema. Men as subjects identifying with agents who drive the film's narrative forward and women are regarded as objects for masculine desire and fetishistic gazing. All of these viewpoints were directed against the representation of women depicted as stereotypes. Scholars like Marjorie Rosen and Molly Haskell are of the opinion that the women are portrayed in Hollywood as madonas, whores, vamps, bimbos, scatterbrains, gold diggers, school teachers, nags and sex kittens etc. Annette Kuhn also emphasizes the same point as she writes: "Arguments have been put forward regarding, for example, certain kind of stereotypical images of women marketed via women's magazines, television advertisements, and other media" (5). The women in films had fixed images because of this misrepresentation; the feminist film critics came forward and lobbied to represent women in a more favorable and positive light. They reacted against the objectification of women in the films. They argued that women are constructed around the visible criteria of beauty and attractiveness. Kuhn further says, "This analysis of images of women is represented as object-victims, particularly in media specially addressed to male audiences" (6).

Feminist film scholars not only presented women in a favorable light but also felt the need to change the basic structure of cinema. They targeted their attention to patriarchy, which was the driving force behind the creation of visual imagery. They focused attention to understand and analyze the dynamics of male chauvinistic film industry. An effort is made towards the construction of alternative, for example, creation of 'strong' female characters. In this chapter film texts the *Earth* and the *Water*, are studied under the scanner of feminist film theory.

Key Concepts of Feminist Film Theory

The debate is opened around feminist film theory. The attention is focused on feminism as a viewpoint which shapes, frames, informs and transforms certain types of film analysis. At this point of time the emphasis is on knowing what feminism does to film theory. In this context, a useful distinction is to be made between feminism as a perspective and feminism as a methodology. In this regard, Kuhn writes:

> Feminism might be regarded on the one hand as a way of seeing the world, a frame of reference or a standpoint from which to examine whatever one wishes to examine. Or alternatively it might be seen as constituting a set of conceptual tools, a method or series of methods, even an analytical model, by means of which to examine its object: in this case film. (67-68)

Feminist film theory embodies in it the multifaceted character of feminism. The methodologies adopted are from within or outside the sphere of feminism. The first of its kind has its origin from socio-cultural roots. Kuhn observes that sociologically based methods would locate images, roles and representations of women in cinema as phenomena reflecting or perhaps determined by, the position of women the 'real' world or the wider society. Explaining further she adds: "Here therefore the main focus of interest has been the ways in which woman has been constituted as a set of meanings through processes of cinematic signification" (69).

In the present chapter, the film texts *Earth* and *Water* are first analyzed based on these models before proceeding to psychoanalytical analysis. Feminist film theory is directed to look at socio-cultural products and institutions led by patriarchal society which conspired to exclude women's voice in the films. Talking about silences of film texts in relation to women, Angela Martin asserts, "the exclusion of woman's voice and her position within the text as object" (12). The focus lies on highlighting how women's voice is silenced despite being shown excessively. Socio-cultural forces dominated by patriarchal society converted women to mere objects. Feminist film theorists tried to draw attention to matters which go unnoticed in the film text. Divulging about the women's presence and absence in the films, Kuhn states:

> These matters are entered not only around presences-the

> explicit ways in which women are represented, the kinds of images, roles constructed by films-but also about absences-the ways in which women do not appear at all or are in certain ways not represented in films. Given the argument that in the sexist society both presences and absences may not be immediately discernible to the ordinary spectator, if only because certain representations appear to be quite ordinary and obvious, then the fundamental project of feminist film analysis can be said to centre on making visible the invisible. (Kuhn 71)

What she suggests is that we as ordinary readers are not able to find the underlying absence of women despite being captured by the camera for a longer duration. Making visible the invisible focuses the attention of reading the film text by pointing to the ways in which women are constructed in film media. Feminist film theory works at dual level of text as well as context. Place and Burton express a similar idea. According to them, the feminist film theory should "Develop and use analysis of our culture that includes a political perspective, knowledge of political conditions, and the role of ideology. Second, feminist [theory] must be both able and willing to analyze films themselves. The entire dynamics of narrative structure must be considered and the tools for comprehending films must be utilized by the feminist critic" (56). In this connection several things are to be taken into consideration while studying the film texts in the purview of feminist film theory. Julia Lesage another writer asserts: "A good theory includes an explanation of the mechanisms operating within the film (form, content. etc.) and the mechanisms that go beyond the product that is the film such as the film industry, distribution, audience, expectoration etc."(13). With the passage of time, Feminist Film Theory grew considerably giving birth to several concepts centering round the portrayal of women as objects and disempowered members and subjected to man's desires. In this regard, Gillion Swanson, feminist film theorist states that since the early eighties, the spectators have become a key centre of debate in feminist film theory especially woman spectator.

But the most-quoted film theorists is Laura Mulvey, who in her essay, *Visual Pleasure and Narrative Cinema*, introduced the concept of the gaze to describe how Hollywood cinema typically assumes a male perspective in the cinematic process. Because of this mode of viewing, the treatment of films in general and women in particular always had patronizing and erotic undertones.

According to Mulvey, there are three basic types of gazing or looking. The first is that of the camera as it records what happens in the film. The second is that of the audience as they watch the film and identify with the main character. The third is that of the characters as they deal and interact with each other in the course of the film. In all three types of looking, the look originates from a masculine point of view. This assigns the role of the active looker and storyteller to the male gender, thus giving them power or control within the movie. Women, on the other hand, are forced to take the passive and therefore powerless role of the one being looked at. They are relegated to just being the object of the male gaze.

The feminist film theory must not be confused with film criticism as it often is. However, there are some overlaps between the two disciplines. It was as early as 1900s, French philosopher Henry Bergson in his *Matter and Memory,* anticipated the development of film theory. It was the time film has been a nascent art born a couple of decades ago. Ever since from its inception in the 1970s, feminist film theory, has revolutionized the way that film and their spectators could be understood. Since then it has become a large and flourishing field. The idea of feminist film theory emerges from the concept that women are left out in the films. They lack their voice and their point of view is not heard. As Sharon Smith, in the first issue of *Women and Film* writes that women, in any full human form, have almost completely been left out of film. She is of the opinion that women are represented merely as objects only to be looked at. Similarly, Naome Gilbert brings to light the notion of the female image as representing the male 'other', having no identity of her own.

The female is portrayed with an archetypal ambivalence. The "Eternal Feminine" has been aesthetically more a principle for realizing male objectives than a person in her own right. Thus the dynamic of myth and reality when converging upon female aesthetic has been quintessentially objectifying... the terms of female aesthetichave been imposed on the basis of man's fears and desires. (Christine Gledhill 93)

In male-dominated, cinematic culture, a woman is represented as a man desires her to be. Despite being over spectacled she is largely absent. The women are identified with the roles assigned to them such as child woman, whore, bitch, wife, mother, secretary, cold and frigid career woman. In this regard, Sholini Chaudhuri writes:

> Since its inception in the 1970s, feminist film theory has provided the impetus for some of the most exciting developments in film studies. "Feminist film theory became the orthodoxy of film theory; such was its influence in the field. Its impact began to be felt in film making itself, with a number of avant- garde and independent and some main stream films linking theory to practice". (1)

It was the women's movement which gave a spark to the feminist film theory. The early film feminist theory centered round the power and function of images. Betty Friedan in her book *The*

Feminine Mystique (1963) emphasized that woman is presented stereotypically conditioned in their own subjugation. Similarly Jan Rosenberg in her book, *Women's Reflections: The Feminist Film Movement,* proposes that a critique of patriarchal representation of women was the core of both mainstream and radical feminist theory. The same idea was propounded by film theorists such as Laura Mulvey, Kaja Silverman, Teresa de Lauretis, and Barbara Creed who opened up a new and distinctive approach to study the films. Their works passionately advocated the important issues of feminism in the films. The feminist film theorists of the time were influenced by civil rights movements, anti-imperialism, anti-colonialism, gay-liberation, and counter-culture. These ideas energized women who lived in these times. Laura Mulvey chronicles this development in a 1989 edition of *Camera Obscura* that historicizes feminist film theory through the memoirs of some of its founding practitioners:

> Feminist use of the new theory and its application to popular culture grew directly out of women's movement's concern with images, their contribution to fixing the connotations of gender and circulating images of women as signifying a patriarchal mythology of sexuality. (23)

In this chapter the concept of male gaze in relation to the film the *Earth* and the *Water* is analytically discussed. The concept of male gaze emerges from Freud's 'Three *Essays on Sexuality*'. He isolated scopophilia as one of the component instinct of sexuality. Writing about Freud's view Laura Mulvey says: "At this point he associated scopophilia with taking other people as objects, subjecting them to a controlling and curious gaze" (Mulvey748). It offers spectators a wish for pleasurable looking gaze what we call as voyeuristic phantasy. The film offers a wonderful spectacle of a brilliant shifting pattern of sound and sight sitting in the darkness of the auditorium promoting an illusion of voyeuristic separation. Film satisfies a primordial wish to look at pleasurable looking objects. Another theorist Jacques Lacan describes scopophilia in its narcissistic aspect. Describing Lacan's view of ego Mulvey writes about him: "Jacques Lacan has described how the moment the child recognizes its own image in the mirror is crucial for the constitution of ego" (Mulvey 749).From here originates "I" of subjectivity. "Hence it is the birth of long love affair/despair between image and self image which has found such intensity of expression in film and such joyous recognition in the cinema audience" (Mulvey749). There are two contradictory aspects of the pleasurable structures of looking at film in a conventional cinematic situation.

> The first, scopophilic, arises from pleasure in using another person as an object of sexual stimulation through sight. The second, developed through narcissism and the constitution of the ego, comes from identification with the image seen. Thus, in film terms, one implies a separation of the erotic identity of the subject from the object on the screen (active scopophilia), the other demands identification of the ego with the object on the screen through the spectator's fascination with and recognition of his like. The first is a function of sexual instincts, the second of the ego libido. (Mulvey 750)

Due to this mode of viewing, women's portrayal is given erotic color. Mulvey is of the opinion that there are two ways of viewing women in the films. The first is the voyeuristic view which emphasizes that women are largely sexualized objects of the male desire. Male looker derives pleasure in observing women without being observed in return. The second view is the fetishistic view wherein the woman, while still being a sexualized objects, has become untouchable. She is glamorized excessively and is put on as a sexual object of auction for male protagonist and of the audience. Fredric Jameson echoes similar views when he says that the visual is essentially pornographic. He is of the opinion that one who is onlooker derives pleasure looking at women characters as sexual objects. He further says that the films ask us to stare at the world as if it were a naked body. He declares that the very act of translating words into photographic images involves a move toward something bodily and nasty. He expresses the same idea as that of Laura Mulvey. Ever since this revolutionary essay by Mulvey, women film makers are endeavoring to counter the male gaze. Not only in Hollywood movies but also in Bollywood films, the woman and her body, is the object of male desire and the source of his viewing pleasure. Women are represented as prizes in almost all visual arts especially in films; women are reduced to nothing but prizes.

For a very long time, women were not characters in their own right. They had stereotyped images such as princess locked in tower, the damsel in distress, the ailing queen, and beautiful girl offered as prize to the hero by her father or guardian offered as a payment for hero's service. But at occasions a hero might possess the object of his desires. In that case this prize is offered to someone else. In most of the films, women are used as show pieces in the films. Ever since its birth, cinema is dominated by men. Women's bodies have been used as decorative pieces. Films are able to make business by showing women as the objects of male desire with their perky legs, bouncy breasts.

Women in Deepa's films are not merely decorative pieces, they are fighters. They do fight with all their grit and gumption. They refuse to submit. Be it Ayah and Lenny in the film *Earth* or Shakuntala, Kalyaniand Chuyia in the film *Water.* They are all fighters.

In visual texts especially in films female sexuality is shown as evil while male sexuality is celebrated. Women are shown as Femme

Fatale distracting the heroes using their vamp sexuality. Men are cautioned against such female sexuality. By contrast, men are depicted differently. The final saviour in the films is always shown as the man. As in the film *Water*, it is not Shakuntala who rescues Chuyia but it is Narayan (John Abraham) in whose arms Chuyia is shown safe and secure. Another way of looking at films is the 'Female Gaze'. It is defined as a work of art presented from female perspective. It reflects female attitudes, either because of the creator's gender or because it is deliberately aimed at female audience. But it does not mean to look at attractive and sexy men. Objectification of women is different from the objectification of men. As Dodai Stewart in her article 'The Male Gaze vs. Female Gaze' writes:

> The objectification of men is a false equivalency to the objectification of women, because what's being fetishized is *strength,* Virility, capability, vigour, fortitude, p*ower.* In a world where men *actually do have power.* You can't say the same about the standard objectification of women, which usually revolves around sexually-charged parts like breasts and buttocks, not biceps. In addition, "sexy" images of women generally involve us being relaxed, lying down, finger in the mouth like a child. Submissive, pliant, docile. (mscinephile.kinja.com)

Attempts have been made to mark out the importance of feminine subjective positions. To recognize feminine desire is also taken under consideration in feminist film theories.

In the film *Earth* all major male characters are shown virile, strong and powerful. All are involved in some form of violence. Be it Dil Nawaz, Hassan, Cook, Mr. Singh, Co. Barucha etc. Ice-Candy-Man exhibits his male potency and vigour. He laid bare his aggression while kidnapping Ayah. The theories advocating female gaze or female spectatorship are rare. Since, women have been advocating for equality, some are talking about corresponding female gaze in which women would be objectifying men and subjecting them to their desires and pleasures. There are certain hindrances in conceptualization of this idea. Mary Ann Doane in her essay 'Film and the Masquerade: Theorizing the female Spectator opines:

> After all, even if it is admitted that the woman is frequently the object of the voyeuristic and fetishistic gaze in the cinema, what is there to prevent her from reversing the relation and appropriating the gaze for her own pleasure? Precisely the fact that the reversal itself remains locked within the same logic. The male striptease, the gigolo-both inevitably signifies the mechanism of reversal itself, constituting themselves as aberrations whose acknowledgement simply reinforces the dominant system of aligning sexual differences with a subject/ object dichotomy. (761)

Ever since 1960s, the 'Feminist Film Theory' has come a long way. There are still very few female directors who came under the influence of feminist film theory while making their films. But still there are few women directors who focused their attention on the issues relevant to women. Some film such as *Boys's Don't Cry* (1999) and *Working Girls* (1986) are kinds of films which represent the complex issues of lesbianism, sexuality and prostitution. These types of films address women's issues. Deepa Mehta's film *Fire*, *Earth* and *Water* are also women centered. *Earth* takes into account the issues of rapes, abduction during the times of partition. The film *Water* is about widowhood and even forced prostitution. Many critics say that Deepa's 108 minutes film *Fire* is about lesbianism inspired from Ismat Chugtai's 1942 story, *Lihaaf* (The Quilt). It was one of the first mainstream films showing homosexual relations.

The feminist film theory argues almost all issues concerning women. This film too deliberates one such issue of homosexuality prevalent in Indian society. The film is about Radha (Shabana Azmi) and Sita (Nandita Das), both neglected by their husbands. They find solace in each other's arms and become lovers. They continue their relations and realize their love for each other. When Ashok came to know about this relation he is horrified and bitter argument goes between them and during this acrimony Radha's sari catches fire. Ashok doesn't bother to put out the fire and steps aside. He let her burn for her sinful desires. She puts out the flames and leaves Ashok. The film came to an end with Radha and Sita joining. The issue the film argues about was so far considered a taboo in Indian societies. Film *Fire* ends up with raising a very signifiant point that assertion of sexual choice is perhaps a necessary condition for the émancipation of women. With in the Framework of *Feminist Film Theory*, *Fire* asserts that free sexual choice is necessary for women's liberation. Deepa Mehta felt pained and expressed frustration in interviews that the film was described as a lesbien film. Manish Deshpande quotes Deepa Mehta : 'Lesbianism is just another aspect of the film...*Fire* is not a film about lesbians," but rather about 'the choices we make in life.' (4)

This chapter focuses to apply these approaches with respect to *Water* and *Earth*, the film by Deepa Mehta. Laura Mulvey in her essay *Visual Pleasure and Narrative Cinema* writes: "In a world ordered by sexual imbalance, pleasure in looking has been split between active/male and passive/ female. The determining male gaze projects its phantasy on to the female figure which is styled accordingly. In their traditional exhibitionist role women are simultaneously looked at and displayed, with their appearance coded for strong visual and erotic impact so that they can be said to connote *to-be-looked-at-ness*" (Mulvey750).

Expressing about masculinity, Warren Blumenfield says that

when we are assigned the designation "male" at the time of birth, the life-long process of "masculinization" starts. It makes us to realize that we are athletic, independent, assertive, domineering, competitive, tough and worthy of respect and pride. Search for any sign of "femininity" and destroy it. This notion clearly presents society's devaluation of females. This attitude of society towards women is to put them down. But there are women film makers such as Deepa Mehta and Meera Nair who are always fervent to represent the true spirit of the women in their films.

Films *Earth* and *Water*: Under the Lens of 'Male Gaze'

Let us put both these film texts under the lens of male gaze. The male gaze is a concept coined by feminist film theorist, Laura Mulvey in her essay '*Visual Pleasure and Narrative Cinema*' in 1975. It discussed the role of women in the films and boldly stated that women are often portrayed as objects. They are portrayed like a commodity to be sold. The viewing of female image results from physiological needs of male spectators. Expressing similar views about male gaze, Maria X Liu writes: "Women are always given meaning how male character views her. She exists purely as spectacle for both the male character and male viewer, with no meaning with herself" (huttingtonpost.com).The concept of male gaze theory is applicable not only in films but in other arts also. "Though it was introduced as a part of film theory, the term can and is often applied to other media. It is often used in critiques of advertisements, television, and the fine arts" (finallyfeminist.com). There are differences between male and female spectators to look at each other. In this regard John Berger writes that men look at women. Women watch themselves being looked at. This determines not only most relations between men and women but also the relation of women to themselves.

Laura Mulvey is of the opinion that men mostly control the camera. She furthers says that women were 'the *bearer of meaning and not the maker of meaning.* 'The statement given by her suggests that women are not assigned the role to control the scene. They are merely something to be looked at. She further believes that there is inequality in viewing that enforces the notion, '*men do the looking, and women are to be looked at.*' All arts are created around a masculine viewer. It is a viewing tendency in visual culture to depict the women from men point of view.Women in the film are objectified. Camera stays focused on a females' body longer than required by the storyline. Even in the advertisements, women are scantily clad for no apparent reasons. These things are connected to what is male gaze theory. Hence it is said that looking is not a neutral activity. Looking is socially constructed. Marita Sturken and Lisa Cartwright assert: 'Through looking we negotiate social relationships and meaning. Looking is a practice much like speaking, writing, or signing. Looking involves learning to interpret and, like other practices, looking involves relationship of power" (10).What they mean to say is that men are presented as lookers and women to be looked at. There are certain cultural codes that are associated with looking or watching. Camera lens acts as a male surrogate. The films are constructed assuming heterosexual male as an observer and female to be observed. The pleasure in looking and desire to fulfill the sexual needs and pleasures of heterosexual viewer. Women too can find pleasure in watching but only if they observe as if they were men. This puts women as being passive object of the male heterosexual as an active subject. According to Laura Mulvey, narrative film is made for the pleasure of male spectator alone, who, "indirectly" possess the female through the look, or rather the relay of looks created by the camera, the male star's gaze, and the spectator's own gaze. The women are the bearer of "the burden of male desire," which is "born with language" (GaylynStudler783). In male dominated sexist society women are socially constructed as 'other' or 'outsider' in sexist society.

Ayah (Nandita Das) in the Film *Earth*: An Object of 'Male Gaze'

In the film *Earth,* the main female character, Ayah is always looked at by the male gaze. Her body movements are displayed for the male's visual pleasure. Her presence accentuates her to be an object for men's sexual gratification. The woman is shown to be endowed with physical assets. The male is supposed to seek pleasure from looking awhile woman does have power to attract men. Ayah is like an aesthetic object of the male characters. Ayah's role in the film is a good example falling within the concept of the Male Gaze Theory. The idea of male gaze centers round the concept that visual arts are created to please heterosexual male audience. Our culture and society do offer males the privilege to look. This aggression of, male gaze is threatening and intrusive. Women are trained in different cultures not to look males directly but avert their eyes. Like film *The Wolf of the Wall Street*, Naomi Lapaglia, the main female character is introduced to the viewers in a very distinctive way. Camera pans her entire figure, paying special attention to her skin tight dress, we hear one of the male characters mutter, and 'I' would let her give me AIDS.' This is one among several such lewd responses. This is made explicit in French Nineteenth century etiquette books that women must avoid looking people in the eye especially men who pass near them. This would be mark of incivility and impudence. While proper women are trained to avert their eyes, courtesan looking directly.

The girls are constructed at young age to see themselves to be looked at. The male to look, for most women the daily experience of such aggressive attention by the male gaze is seen to be threatening and intrusive. Emile Zola in his novel *Nana*, published in 1880 and whose main character was a courtesan, writes: "Nana looked all the ladies in the face, and made a point of staring hard at the Comtesse Sabine."Shohini Chaudhary illuminating the idea of Mulvey's male gaze argued that the controlling gaze in cinema is always male. She asserts that the spectators identify themselves with the male hero and the heroine is an object of erotic spectacle and men and women are differently positioned by cinema. Men as subjects identifying with heroes who drive the narrative forward and the women an object for masculine desire and fetishistic gazing. Modleski is of the opinion that Mulvey's theory is regarded as the founding document of feminist film theory. Male fancies and pleasures are given importance at the cost of a woman's body. In the film *Earth* Ayah is viewed by male gaze as a sexual object. Wherever she walks, talks and stops she is looked as an object of sexual desire. Even the stub-handed beggars do not lag behind. As Sidhwa writes:

Up and down, they look at her. Stub-handed twisted beggars and dusty old beggars on crutches drop their poses and stare at her with hard, alert eyes. Holy men, masked in piety, shove aside their pretences to ogle her with lust. Hawkers, cart drivers, cooks, coolies and cyclists turn their heads as she passes. (ICM 3)

Wherever Ayah moves, covetous eyes always followed her. Ayah is watched by all her admirers with passionate desire. A warm flood of stares is always directed at her by all her admirers be it the Ice-candy-man, the Fallettis Hotel Cook, the Government House Gardener, Masseur or Sher Singh. All get attracted towards her and Lenny has full confidence in Ayah's chocolate chemistry to have a magnetic effect on all those. The film shows how Ayah's body is dehumanized solely based on the body during both in love and chaos.

In *Earth*, the greedy male gaze towards Ayah's body is

captured in the park scene where male admirers from different religious communities (Hindu, Muslim, and Sikhs) sit circling Ayah. When her Sari slips unconsciously from her chest, exposing her breast partially, all the men are taken aback and kept looking at her breast with silent lust and desire. Besides male gaze, rape is another instrument used in the film to dehumanize women. The rapes in the film *Earth* originated not out of carnal lust or desire, but from the idea of degrading the weaker (woman) to have an irreparable impact on the other (man). The women are raped, mutilated and impregnated to pollute the bloodline of a particular community. However, this horrifying tale of atrocity meted out to women of both communities comes in minuscule, yet in a powerful way. The film depicts Lenny and cousin talk to some unnamed little boy who tells about the discovery of his mother's naked body.

Kalyani (Lisa Ray): An Object of Male Gaze in the Film *Water*

Not only Ayah but Kalyani too is portrayed as object of male gaze in the film *Water.* In the film text the *Water*. She too is treated nothing more than a sexual object. In the film she is portrayed wearing white *sari,* exposing her round limbs. Kalyani too is object of male gaze. Ever since the priest Sadanand has assumed his duties as a young priest, he has been attracted by the widows. He lusted for their flesh. "He lusted for the young, the middle-aged and, except for the old, even the elderly" (Water 79). This is male gaze; even the priest fancies to bury his face in their necks. He simply cannot resist the voluptuous joggle of their flesh. And the eroticism of these religious hawks was heightened by vulnerability and availability of widows. He justifies this by saying that if the Gods lusted and got what they wanted, how was he, a puny mortal, to resist the allure of these women? Kalyani is forced into prostitution.

Her body is used not only a sex-object but an object of exchange. She is forced into prostitution. In this regard Maureen Turim asserts: "The female body is not only a sex-object, but also an object of exchange; its value can be sold (prostitution) or it can be incorporated in to another commodity which can be sold" (56)

Shakuntala (Seema Biswas) in *Water*: A Portrayal as an Object of 'Male Gaze'

Shakuntala is another middle aged widow in the film *Water.* She too is an object of male gaze. She is constantly watched by Sadanand, the priest.

He idly watched Shakuntala fill the pot and walk up the ghats with holy water. As the light shone through her damp sari, it outlined her thighs and legs. It gave him pleasure to watch her. Not for the first time, he observed the grace in her strong, shapely body. Her waist was slender above the rounded flare of her hips, her stomach flat. Her high breasts made shapely mounds beneath her handsome shoulders, and her neck sat straight above the indentations of her collar bones; he wished he could bury his lips in the hollows.(Water 156)

When Kalyani commits suicide, the void created by her is to be filled by Chuyia. The process of patriarchal brutality will continue. Mehta uses sound effects, actor's expression and other filmic instruments to give graphic details to the audience to expose the double standard of male dominated society. Such is the male gaze. Even the priest could not resist her bodily charm. As Shakuntala stood up and her sari got pinched in the cleft between her buttocks."Sadanand had an almost irresistible urge to pry it out, and at the same time he feasted his eyes on the shape the round globes of her buttocks made" (Water157). Describing Ayah, Lenny says that her presence galvanizes men to mad sprints in noon heat. Muvley in her celebrated essay '*Visual Pleasure and Narrative Cinema*' narrates that male acts an agent of the look and the female as an object of spectacle through the mechanism and voyeurism and fetishism. Feminist film theory certainly enriches our experience about films, provides us with many tools for analysis and regards women not 'just the sources of entertainment', but as humans with all their strengths and weaknesses. They are not mere showpieces.

Conclusion

In this book an attempt has been made to understand novel and film as two different mediums and their corresponding shift to one another; novel into film and vice versa. The argument in this book centered round four texts; two novels by Sidhwa and two films by Mehta respectively, former as a novelist and latter as a film maker.

Sidhwa and Mehta seem to act in collaboration. Mehta's film the *Earth*'s an adaptation of the novel *Ice-Candy-Man* whereas Sidhwa wrote a novel *Water* based on a film of the same name by the former. The debate on cinematic adaptations, fidelity to the original source, divergence, novelization, stigma of borrowing, sticking to the internal logic, maintaining of the 'spirit' of the novel and the film in case of novelization are scrutinized in detail. Next important aspect taken under study was to evaluate the proposed four texts in feminine perspective. Feminism and its all – embracing facets including its origin from stone age, three waves of feminism, voices of great feminists, Sidhwa and Mehta's views in their novels and films especially in the proposed text were also incorporated in the study. Some light was also thrown to highlight the intertextuality of these texts. And the four texts are studied in a feminist approach and finally the film text the *Earth* and the

Water are put under the lens of feminist film theory. After an exhaustive and extensive study of Chapter-I '*Ice-Candy-Man* and *1947: Earth*: A Hybrid Presentation of Literary and Visual Texts'. The following conclusions are arrived at:

Bapsi Sidhwa and Deepa Mehta are artists having some divine association. Both are influenced with each other and have a unique trust strengthened by some spiritual conviction. At the outset an attempt was made to know about both Sidhwa and Mehta and their artistic affiliation. Interestingly some similarities bind them together. Sidhwa being a Pakistan born diasporic writer and Mehta is India born diasporic film maker. Both are fighters in their own rights, voicing for the common cause concerning women. The film *Earth* is a cinematic cousin of the novel *Ice-Candy-Man*. Both the texts tell the story of partition. It was a huge and daunting task to transform words in to moving images. Mehta has done a commendable job of making *Earth* inspired from the novel *Ice-Candy-Man* with her cinematic tools what we call in cinematic terminology *mise-en-scene.* While transforming one text (novel into a film) into another, an argument about the pros and cons, each media is associated with is taken into consideration to arrive at the conclusion.

It is found that Sidhwa is a neutral observer and gives an objective account of the partition through a girl child Lenny. No doubt that she is absolutely impartial in representing women in *the Ice-Candy-Man* but politically she seems to give an edge to Pakistani perspective of partition. On the other hand, Mehta is born into a Hindu family, is a citizen of Canada. She gives the Indian perspective of partition a little more weight keeping in mind the Indian audience. As far the representation of women is concerned, she too is impartial. Both of them must be given credit in presenting the drama of partition through a feminist perspective with seriousness and honesty.

Sidhwa gives a more elaborate depiction of the turmoil and atrocities being inflicted on women as seen through the eyes of a girl child. This inter-racial harmony turns into bitter hostility and the people around Lenny and Ayah change along racial, political and religious lines and eventually do not hesitate to kill each other. The novel goes slowly and convincingly whereas due to time limits the film moves fast. It was a tough task for Mehta to condense a novel of 277 pages into 101 minute film. Siwhwa's world is open ended. She has exercised a full freedom in writing *Ice-Candy-Man* whereas Mehta had to face many hurdles in making the film *Earth*. Visualization, in itself is a constraint. It narrows down the open ended world of characters, objects, conversations and landscapes and at some places it seems to destroy the subtleties as is created by Sidhwa in the novel. But Mehta has had to deal with innumerable factors most of them not in her control.

Despite many hurdles such as time constraint, budget and censure restrictions, Mehta has successfully upheld the 'spirit' of the novel from where the film is sourced. Even the gentle sex scenes have been were censored which somehow contributed in turning the film a commercial failure despite having a star cast of Amir Khan, NanditaDass and Rahul Khana.Sidhwa has revealed her characters through language employing similes, metaphors, allusions, paradoxes, irony whereas Deepa has revealed them through visual images using uses various cinematic tools such as frame, shot, freeze, fades, colour, light, sound, songs, and voice-overs.

Transposing a character from the pages to the screen is a mammoth task it might not be the exact copy as written by the novelist. The lame Lenny and enthralling Ayah both seem to peep through the pages *of Ice-Candy-Man* as close seem their delineation by Mehta. The film depicts the element of romance during the political upheaval. Ayah-Hassan love is shown in a romantic fervour. And *Ice-Candy-Man* (Aamir Khan), another Muslim youth, her admirer vying for her affection happens to see Ayah-Hassan indulging in passionate love making. This revelation becomes the reason for Hassan's murder. Adaptation of *Ice-Candy-Man* into the film *Earth* is superbly executed.

The cast of the film Maia Sethna, Nandita Dass, Aamir Khan, Rahul Khana, Kulbhushan Kharbanda have done justice in depicting the human drama. A.R.Rehman's music and Javed Akhtar's lyrics made *Earth* a beautiful adaptation. However, while adapting *Ice-Candy-Man* into *Earth* some additions and omissions have been done by Mehta keeping in mind the requirements and limitations of the visual media such as the introduction of voice-over. She has used a female voice of Shabana Azmi for Lenny which sounds: "I was eight years old, living in Lahore in March 1947 when British Empire in India started to collapse. Along with talks of India's Independence from British came rumbling about its division into two countries, Pakistan and India. Hindus, Muslims, and Sikhs who had lived together as one entity for centuries suddenly started to clamor for pieces of India for themselves. The arbitrary line of division to British control to carve up India in August 1947 would scar the sub-continent forever." (Mehta) The film comes to an end with Old Lenny's voice by Shabana Azmi: "Two hundred and fifty years of British Empire ended in 1947. But what is there to show except for a country divided. The massacres and kidnapping vendettas and more violence, was it all worth? Fifty years have gone by since I betrayed my Ayah, Some say she married Ice Candy Man, some say they saw her in a brothel in Lahore, Others they saw her in Amritsar. But I never set eyes on her again. And that day in 1947, when I lost Ayah, I lost large part of myself" (Mehta).

'Voice-over' is a wonderful technique used in film making to compress the idea which otherwise require many pages in the novel. Mehta has done a commendable job in employing this voice-over technique in her novel and squeezed Sidhwa's 277 pages novel into a screenplay of 101 minutes.

The novel gives a detailed account of Lahore of 40s and 50s.It gives a graphic account of Lahore during the years preceding partition. Whereas the film does not delve in detail and simply omits first sixty pages of the novel.

The film comes to an end with Ayah being dragged by a crazy mob led by the man who loves her. The film ends at a point leaving the audience full of question. However, the voice-over by old Lenny (Shabana) does reveal something about Ayah. But Sidhwa has devoted ninety pages to explain what happened to Ayah after she was abducted by the crazy mob. From a film's point of view it is absolutely relevant to make the film end with Ayah's abduction. To leave the audience with some unanswered questions was absolutely fine on the part of a film maker. But a writer cannot leave the readers unanswered. The novel has dealt in detail what happened after Ayah's abduction. Sidhwa's women characters show extraordinary resilience and fortitude to resist male dominance. All her women characters such as Mother, Godmother, Mucho, Slavesister, Hamida and Ayah represent the process of recovery whereas this aspect of recovery is missing in the film. The film focuses on the two aspects, first being the partition of India and the other the violence that followed. Then there are characters who played a vital role in the novel are missing in the film. Godmother, Slavesister, Electric Aunt and Hamida are such characters. After Ayah's abduction, Godmother plays a very a crucial role in the novel. She takes on the charge and fights for Ayah. Though, she was also hostile to Slavesister. A full chapter "Ranna's story" is reduced to a very short and insignificant narrative by a nameless boy. While the chapter 'Ranna's Story' in the novel is very absorbing and agonizing. However, there are some other minor changes in the film such as Masseur gives Ayah a ride in his cycle in place of Sharbat Khan. Another difference is that Ice candy man threatens to drop Lenny suspended from the air instead of her brother Adi. Both these minor changes have been made by Mehta to serve two purposes. Giving a ride by Messeur certainly enhances the romantic aspect whereas threatening Lenny to be dropped, Dil Nawaz (Ice-Candy-Man) snatches some moments to be with Ayah.

Sidhwa is a writer of global eminence and her readers are not confined to the Indian sub-continent only but spread across the world. She wrote *Ice-Candy-Man* (1988) in English but she freely employed Punjabi and Urdu words. It was perfectly all right on the part of Sidhwa to write in a language of global prominence.

Mehta on the contrary has used Hindi as a medium of communication. Unlike a novel which is a medium of literate and elite, film is a mass medium catering to the needs of all. Keeping in mind the audience and economic implications of the film Mehta sticks to Hindi. Like all Hindi films introduced song sequences keeping in mind the popular demand of the Indian audience.

Another important point of difference between the two where the novel seems to score point over the film is the depiction of sexuality especially sexual maturation of Lenny.This is a remarkable attempt on the part of Sidhwa because it is a courageous attempt on the part of woman writer in the country like Pakistan. The novel has certainly depicted the women characters in their individual self. Sidhwa's women are not inert; they show their resentment and act in their own manner whereas the film due to certain limitations of media and time fails to depict them in detail.

The ending of the film is acceptable with the abduction of the Ayah that leaves the spectators awe-struck. They come out of the theatre with thousand questions. The film being a medium of masses, scores a point over the novel because it reaches to the wider chunk of audience whether they are literate or not. After analyzing and evaluating all these points, it can be deduced that an adaptation of *Ice-Candy-Man* by Mehta into the film *Earth* is a great artistic venture. It has remained faithful to the internal logic of the novel and has retained the spirit of the novel

In Chapter-II 'Reading *Water* as Film and Novel', we came across a phenomenon called novelization. It's an uncommon literary practice. The film *Water* written and directed by Deepa Mehta was transformed into a novel of the same name by Sidhwa Wapsi. After an extensive and elaborate analysis the following is concluded.

The first query concluded is what made Sidhwa to write the novel *Water* being inspired by a film of the same name? It was the first query which needed an answer. It was a difficult task to convert a film script into a novel. The prime reason for Sidhwa to write a novel inspired from a film was that she wanted to have an elaborate discussion about the theme undertaken in the film. She wanted to say what remained unsaid in the film because of time constraints the film media is subject to. Sidhwa and Mehta are the admirers of each other. They are in other words voice of women, former through literary text and latter through visual text. They share a common concern for women of the Indian sub-continent and their fight against patriarchal forces. Making of the film *Water* was a mammoth task; it was shrouded in controversy from the very beginning, even before the first scene could be filmed. Mehta was leveled as anti-Hindu and anti-Brahmin. A mob of 2000 attacked and demolished the set and threw the pieces in the Ganges. This chapter is focused on understanding the trials and tribulations Mehta underwent in while making the film. After the complete ban on the film, four years later the film resurrected from scratch with a name '*Full Moon*' in Sri Lanka. But writing of the novel *Water* was a simple affair starting with flair of Sidhwa's pen. In the Making of the film *Water* more than eighty person crew worked in Mini-Benares created with a Sri Lankan river as the Ganga. It took almost a village to make the film *Water* after so many controversies. On the other hand the novel was the outcome of a single person named Bapsi Sidhwa.

The film starts with an eight year old Chuyia riding on a bullock cart with her two tiny, bare feet, encircled with silver anklets, chewing sugar cane. But Sidhwa devoted 23 pages to reach to this point. She depicted in detail the family atmosphere Chuyia grows in. She goes in search of gooseberry and finds Tun-Tun. There is detailed description of the family atmosphere. Somnath-Bhagya conversation regarding Chuyia's marriage to HiraLal is given some detail. This detailed description was given by Sidhwa to explain to the readers who are alien to the concept of widowhood prevalent in the Hindu society. When the film starts, the Western spectator fails to understand the journey of Chuyia to widowhood. Sidhwa illuminates the idea more clearly than the film could because of time constraint. She has done a wonderful job in elaborating Mehta's views.

The film uses camera, which is an impartial device with (high, low, and overhead) to create a particular effect. Whereas novelist's device which is a pen,is never an impartial device, it scribbles lines as are dictated by the writer.

Chuyia's (Sarla) and Shakuntala (Seema Biswas) in the film have done a wonderful job too. Both have done justice to their roles. While watching the film the writer finds that the emotional grip that the film could have created is marred by some poor acting by Liza Ray and John Abraham in the roles of Kalyani and Narayan respectively. Manorama in the role of Madhumati and RaghuvirYadav as Gulabi has done great job. The emotional appeal which seems missing at points in the film is compensated in the novel by Sidhwa by the flair of her pen. The novel said everything which was unsaid in the film.

In writing of the novel *Water* Sidhwa has put her weight behind Deepa Mehta to reinforce the idea propounded by Mehta to bring to the surface the serious issue about the travesties of widows who are forced to live in ashrams away from society. Sidhwa's *Water* is a well written novel lending beauty to the film *Water* from where it has been inspired. It is an extension of Deepa's view which she could not depict because of the time and other constraints beyond her control. It can be concluded that the novel has not been a hatch-work of the film but extension and elaboration of the ideas cinematographed in the film.

Chapter-III 'Feminist Reading of Literary Texts – *Water, Earth* and Film Texts – *Earth, Water*', *Water* the novels and *Earth* and *Water* the films, focused on an argument about feminism in the selected texts. The argument started with exploring the traces of feminism from the Stone Age when there seemed to have equality of gender as both male and female used same implements. But with the dawn of agriculture the imbalance emerged. Men started accumulating resources and with the advent of metal age woman's fate took turn and the defeat of feminine sex was inevitable. The respectable position woman occupied during Stone Age dwindled and she became confined to domestic duties and she came under the control of her husband. She became a property in the patriarchal society. All types of vices were perpetrated on women in the name of religion, culture and tradition. To counter this prejudice, an ideology of feminism emerged. With this, movements advocating women's political, social and economic rights started. The arguments of Kate Millet, Simone de Beauvoir and Mary Wollstonecraft etc. are taken into account while studying all the four texts under consideration.

The elements of feminism are explored in the novel *Ice-Candy-*

Man. The women protagonists, Lenny, Ayah, Godmother, Mother, Kalyani, Chuyia, Shakuntala and even Madhumati all struggle and fight against the patriarchal set up. Sidhwa and Mehta's women characters take on the patriarchal forces head on. They are unwilling to bow down at the altar of patriarchy. All of them exhibit an extraordinary resilience in challenging patriarchal forces in all the selected texts. All sorts of brutalities are inflicted on women. Ayah is abducted, raped and thrown into prostitution. During partition, revenge was inflicted on women's body irrespective of religion. Regardless, all the women characters especially in the novel exhibit an extraordinary courage, resilience and individuality not to be easily subjugated. It is their sheer valour to expose the patriarchal prejudices rampant in the contemporary society.

Presentation of Lenny's sexual maturation is well written by Sidhwa. It is a courageous attempt on her part to bring a gynocentric view in a male chauvinistic society. The beauty of the novel comes through Lenny's growth and sexual maturation. Besides this Ayah and Godmother,two women protagonists display an extraordinary resilience in the wake of utmost brutality being perpetrated by men. *Ice-Candy-Man* and *Earth* are truly feminist texts. In both these texts, Sidhwa very subtly and effectively challenges the deep-rooted elements of patriarchy. Her women characters exhibit extraordinary forbearance, their choices and will along with the feminine qualities of kindness, empathy and motherhood.

In making Lenny as the narrator, Sidhwa puts her weight to validate her feminist point of view. All her women are able to acquire heroic grandeur. Lenny never let her cousin to manipulate her sexually. Ayah is in no mood to forgive *Ice-Candy-Man*. She is rock solid and is an epitome of loyalty to the family she serves. Godmother has an incredible capacity to handle difficult situations. She acts like a scorpion to admonish Ice candy man. She is another woman who stands high and in character, is a glorious example of self confidence and authoritativeness. This is a wonderful text in which women are pitted against patriarchal set up in the times of partition. Sidhwa also brings to surface the suppression of women by women through Godmother-Slavesister relationship.

This chapter also takes into account the feminist reading of the film *Water* and the novel *Water.* Both deal with the issue of widowhood in pre-independent India of 1930s and the awful conditions they are forced to live in. Mehta and Sidhwa, the former with visual images and the later with words expose religious hypocrisy. The film *Water* by Mehta commences with an epigram on the blank screen "A widow should be long suffering until death, self-restrained and chaste. A virtuous wife who remains chaste when her husband dies goes to heaven. A woman who is undutiful to her husband is reborn in the womb of jackal." (The Laws of Manu Chapter 5 verse (156-161) Dharamashastra (Sacred Hindu Text). Inequality and degradation of women is almost sanctified in Hindu religion. Mehta's film *Water* focuses on a very important issue concerning women. It depicts the inhuman conditions the widows are forced to live in the 1930s pre-independent India. This was the time when men were the champions of society and women were not allowed to make their own decisions. Girls were married off in very tender age to older men through arranged marriages. As in the film *Water,* Chuyia a girl of eight is given off in marriage to a man forty four years of age. Deepa Mehta portrays the plight of child widow Chuyia. Undoubtedly, she strikes hard at the existing patriarchy. Her passage into widowhood is tormenting When Chuyia's father declares that her husband is dead and she has become a widow. Chuiya's mother-in-law does not waste time to jerk the *mangalsutra* of fher neck and the beads scattered on the ground. Little Chuyia is shaken. She seized Chuyia's hand and violently smashed the red glass bangles with a piece of brick. After smashing her bangles, another woman pulled down Chuyia's skirt and pulled her blouse up over her neck and instructs how to wear clothes as a widow. Women too are shown not lagging behind in wounding the spirit of women. Kalyani, the young widow who is the only bread winner for the ashram. To look attractive her head is not shaved. She is forced into prostitution to support the ashram. She is caught in the whirlpool of Hindu society People miss no opportunity to disgrace the widow.

Deepa and Sidhwa both strike hard at the phony and untruthful morality prevalent in Hindu society. In *Water* the film, Mehta made an extraordinary attempt to depict the plight of widows in India who yearn for liberation of their body and soul. Kalyani, another victim of Brahminical ideology, is pushed into prostitution. Shakuntala (Seema Biswas) is a middle-aged widow, living in the ashram an enigmatic, considerate and devout Hindu widow is a victim of obsolete Brahminical ideology. She is torn between her religious faith and human desires. She takes on Madhumati, the head widow to save Chuyia as well as Kalyani. She defies Madhumai and frees Kalyani to have her desires fulfill. She is a mother figure to Chuyia. It is Shakuntala who consoles Narayan when Kalyani commits suicide. All the women characters in the select texts such as Lenny, Ayah, Godmother, Chuyia, Shakuntala,Kalyani display the essential qualities of womanhood. Both Sidhwa and Mehta have done a wonderful work in demonstrating the feminist perspectives in the film as well as novel. The researcher regards Sidhwa a little better, though both have played with different tools. The tools Mehta has used are certainly difficult to handle because the film making is far more complex and involves loads of things not just a pen. It is safe to conclude that both the works of art must be treated as a new, independent, coherent and convincing creation with its own meanings.

In Chapter-IV 'Film Texts – *Earth* and *Water*: Under the Lens of Feminist Film Theory', both the film texts are put under the scanner of feminist film theory. The Film theory which began in the 1970s is an integrated study closely associated with psychology, economics and socio-political aspect. In this chapter both the film texts are analyzed on the basis of theories propounded by eminent theorists such as Sergei Eisenstein, Jean Epstein, Andre Bazin and the most importantly Laura Mulvey. One such approach is to study both the film texts under the lens of feminism. This approach gave birth to Feminist film theory. Women so far were depicted in films as stereotypes such as madonas, whores, vamps, bimbos, scatterbrains, gold diggers, school teachers, nags and sex kittens etc. They were associated with fixed images. In fact, they had been misrepresented in the films. But feminist film theorists lobbied to represent women in a more favorable and positive light by giving emphasis to change the basic structure of cinema. They targeted their attention to patriarchy which somehow created visual imagery being influenced by patriarchy. Both the films are studied taking into consideration Laura Mulvey concept of male gaze which fall in three categories: first is that of the camera as it records what happens in the film, second is that of audience gaze, how they identify with and perceive the characters and third is the response of characters as they deal and interact with each other in the course of the film. Jacques Lacan's description of narcissistic aspect and Freud's view to have a pleasure of looking at other without being observed in return is also taken into consideration. Mulvey is of the opinion that there are two ways of viewing women in the films. The first is the voyeuristic view which emphasizes that women are largely sexualized objects of the male desire. The male looker derives pleasure in observing women without being observed in return. The second way is the fetishistic view wherein the woman, while still being a sexualized objects, has become untouchable. She is glamorized excessively and is put on as a sexual object of auction for male protagonist and of the audience. Ever since Mulvey's revolutionary essay women film makers are endeavoring to counter the male gaze. Deepa Mehta in her films the *Earth* and the *Water* has shown characters like Ayah (Nandita Das) Kalyani (Lisa Ray) and Shakuntala (Seema Biswas) not only as the objects of male gaze and the source of viewing pleasure but she has been able to raise them above that and had imparted them the unparallel moral strength. In almost all visual arts especially in films, women are reduced to nothing but 'a prize'. For a very long time, women were not characters in their own right.

But at occasion a hero might possess the object of his desires. In that case this prize is offered to someone else. But contrary to this the film *Earth* by Mehta is a step further to depict women in their own right. Ayah vehemently rejects Ice-candy-man's offer to be taken under his care. Lenny does not allow cousin to be manipulated sexually by him. In the film *Water*, Shakuntala, despite all difficulties does not lose faith in God. She even supports Narayan whose faith in God seems to shake in extreme difficulty. The cinema is dominated by men ever since its birth. Since then women's bodies have been used as decorative pieces. Films are able to make business by showing women as the objects of male desire with their perky legs and bouncy breasts . But the women in Sidhwa's novel *Ice-Candy-Man* and *Earth* and in Mehta's films *Earth* and *Water* are not decorative pieces, they are fighters. They do fight with all their grit and gumption. All of them refuse to submit whether she is Ayah, Shakuntala, Lenny, Chuyiaor Kalyani.

In the final words it can be concluded that Sidhwa and Mehta are artists having some divine association. They seem to supplement each other through their women characters despite having played with different tools, in different environs, in different places and in different times. Both have been successful in communicating pleasingly the critique of feminism through a very unique artistic collaboration of adaptation and novelization.

Works Cited and Consulted

Primary Sources

Books:

Sidhwa, Bapsi. *Ice-Candy-Man.*New Delhi: Penguin Books India, 1988. Print.

The following abbreviation is used for the work of Bapsi Sidhwa in different chapters of the thesis: *ICM: Ice-Candy-Man*

— *Water.*New Delhi: Penguin Books India, 2006. Print.

Primary Sources:

Films:

1947: Earth. Deepa Mehta. Perf.Aamir Khan, NanditaDass, Maia Sethna, Kitu Gidwani, Arif Zakaria, Kulbhashan Kharbanda, Pawan Malhotra, Rajender Kumar and Rahul Khana. New Yorker Films, 1998.DVD.

*Water.*Deepa Mehta. Perf. Seema Biswas, Lisa Ray, John Abraham, Sarla Kariyawasam, Manorama, Waheeda Rehman, Raghuvir Yadav and Kulbhushan Kharbanda. Universum Film, 2005. DVD.

Secondary Sources:

Films:

Charulata.Satyajit Ray. Perf. Madhabi Mukharjee, Soumitra Chatterjee, Sailen Mukhharjee. Blu-Ray, 2013. DVD.

Finzan.Sissoko, Cheick Omar. Perf. Diarrah Sanago, Sadou Touru, Namory Keita, BalaMousa, Koti. NTCS Colour Broadcast System.Bambara:2008. DVD.

Fire.Deepa Mehta. Perf. Shabana Azmi, Nandita Das, Kulbhushan Kharbanda and Javed Zafri, Ranjit Chowdhary and Devyani Saltzman.Kaleidoscope Entertainment, 1996.DVD.

Pather Panchali. Satyajit Ray. Perf. Subir Banerjee, Kanu Banerjee, Karuna Banerjee, Uma Dasguta, Tulsi Chakarvarti. Sony Pictures Classics, 1995.DVD.

Pinjar. Chanderparkash Dwivedi. Perf. Urmila Matondkar, Manoj Bajpei, Sanjay Suri, Piyanshu Chatterjee, Sandali Sinha, Isha Kopikar. Blu-Ray, 2010. DVD.

The Circle. Panhi, Jafar. Perf. Fereshteh Sadre, Nargess Mamizadeh, FatehmehNaghavi, Solmaz Panahi, MaedehTamasebi.Blu-Ray.2010.DVD.

The Piano. Jane Campion. Perf. Holly Hunter, Harvey Keitel, Sam Neil, Anna Paquim. Blu-Ray Netflisx, 1993. DVD.

The Train to Pakistan.Rook, Pamela. Perf.Nirmal Pandey, RajitKapur, Mohan Agashe, Smriti Mishra. Blu-Ray.2010. DVD.

Secondary Sources

Books:

Abrams, M.H. *A Glossary of Literary Terms*.1993. Bangalore: Prism, 2011. Print.

Barry, Peter. "Feminist Criticism."*Beginning Theory: An Introduction to Literary and Cutural Theory*. New Delhi. Viva Books, 2010. Print

Barthes, Roland. *The Theory of the Text Untying the Text: A Post Structural Reader.* Ed.Robert Young. London: Routledge, 1981. Print.

Basu, Amrita, "Feminism Inverted: The Gendered Imagery and Real Woman of Hindu Nationalism." *Women and Right Wing Movements: Indian Experiences.*ed. Tanika Sarkar and Urvashi Butalia.London: Zed, 1995. Print.

Beauvoir, Simone. *The Second Sex.* London: Vintage Books, 1997. Print.

Bluestone, George. "The Limits of the Novel and the Limits of the Film."*Novels into Film.* 3rd ed. Baltimore: Johns Hopkins Press, 2003. Print.

Butalia, Urvashi. *The Other Side of Silence.* New Delhi: Viking, 1998. Print.

Chaudhary, Shohini. *Feminist Film Theorists: Laura Mulvey, Kaja Silverman, Teresa de Lauretis, BarbaraCreed.*London: Routledge Taylor & Francis Group, 2006. Print.

Cohen, Keith. *Film and Fiction: The Dynamics of Exchange.* New Haven: Yale University Press: 1979. Print.

Desmond, John, and Peter Hawkes. *Adaptation: Studying Film and Literature.* New York: McGraw Hill. 2006. Print.

Desai, Neera, and UshaThakkar. *Women in Indian Society.* National Book Trust of India: New Delhi, 2001. Print.

Dhawan, R.K, and Novi Kapadia."The Fiction of BapsiSidhwa" *The Novels of BapsiSidhwa.*New Delhi: Prestige Books. 1996. Print.

Dominelli, Louis. *Anti-racist Social Work: A Challenge for White Practioners and Educators.* Basingstoke: Mac Milan, 1988. Print.

Doniger, Wendy, and Brian K. Smith, *The Laws of Manu.* Harmondsworth: Penguin Books, 1991. Print.

Durrani, Tehmina. *Blasphemy.* New Delhi: Penguin Books, 1999. Print.

Eagleton, Terry. *The English Novel: An Introduction*. Oxford: London 2005. Print.

Hammer, Robert D. *Joseph Conrad: Third World Perspective*. Washington: The Three Continents Press, 1990. Print.

Jaidka, Manju. *A Critical Study of Deepa Mehta's Trilogy: Fire, Earth and Water*. New Delhi: Readsworthy, 2011. Print.

Gopal, Sangit, and Sujata Moorti.*Global Bollywood: Travels of Hindi Song and Dance*. Minnesota Press. 2008. Print.

Hutcheon, Linda. *A Theory of Adaptation*. New York: Routledge. 2006. Print.

Kuhn, Annette. "Making Visible the Invisible."*Women's Pictures: Feminism and Cinema*. 3rd ed. London: Verso, 1994. Print.

Macdonald, Gina, and Andrew. E. Macdonald. *Jane Austen on Screen*.Cambridge: Cambridge University Press. 2003. Print

McFarlane, Brian. *Novels to film:An Introduction to the theory of Adaptation*. Oxford: Claredon Press. 1996. Print.

McLuhan, Marshall. *Understanding Media: The Extensions of Man*. New York: McGraw-Hill, 1964. Print.

Martin, Angela. *Notes on Feminism and Films*.Unpublished discussion paper, British Film Institute. 1976. Print.

Pike, David L. *Canadian Cinema since 1980s: At the Heart of the World*. Toronto: University of Toronto Press, 2012. Print.

Rao, Raja. *The Serpent and the Rope*. Delhi: Orient Paperbacks, 1960. Print.

Singh, Gokul. *Popular Culture in a Globalized India*.Taylor & Francis.2009. Print.

Tay, Sharon Lin. "On the Edges of Post-Colonialism:Deepa Mehta and Transnational Cinema." *In Women on the Edge: Twelve Political Film Practices*. New York: Palgrave Macmillan, 2009. Print.

Wagner, Geoffrey. *The Novel and the Cinema*. Rutherford, NJ: Farleigh Dickinson University Press. 1975. Print.

Wexman, Virginia Wright.“ Birth and Childhood of a New Art.” *A History of Film.*6th ed.Delhi: Dorling Kindersley, 2007. Print.

Wollstonecraft, Mary. *A Vindication of Rights of Women*. London: Vintage Books. 2014. Print.

Wood, Michael. *Film: A Very Short Introduction.* Oxford: Oxford University Press, 2012. Print.

Articles in Books

Asaduddin, M, and AnuradhaGhosh.“ Some Reflections and a Brief History.” *Filming Fiction.*1sted. New Delhi: Oxford University Press. 2012. Print.

Cartmell, Deborah, and Imelda Whelehan. *Adaptations: From Text to Screen, Screen to Text.* New York: Routeledge, 1999. Print.

Chakravarti, Uma “Gender, Caste, and Labour: The Ideological and Material Structure of Widowhood.” *Widows in India: Social Neglect and Public Action,* ED. Martha Alter Chen, New Delhi: Sage Publications, 1998. Print.

Chatman, Seymour. “What Novels Can Do That Film Can’t (And Vice Versa). *Film Theory and Criticism.*4th Ed. Mast Gerald, Marshall Cohen, Leo Braudy. New York: Oxford University Press.1992. Print.

Doane, Mary Ann. ‘Film and the Masquerade: Theorising the Female Spectator” *Film Theory and Criticism.* Ed. Gerald Mast, Marshall Cohen, Leo Braudy. 4th ed. New York: Oxford University Press. 1992. Print.

Gledhill, Christine. “ Recent Developments in Feminist Criticism.” *Film Theory and Criticism: Women and Represention.* Ed. Gerald Mast, Marshall Cohen, Leo Braudy. 4th ed. New York: Oxford University Press. 1992. Print.

Kent and Joe Gotler.“ Exploiting Book- Publishing Rights.” *Movie*

*Business Book.*Ed. Jason E. Squire, Maidenhead: McGraw Hill, 1994. Print.

Mulvey, Laura. " Visual Pleasure and Narrative Cinema." *Film Theory and Criticism.*Ed. Gerald Mast, Marshall Cohen, Leo Braudy. 4th Ed. New York: Oxford University Press. 1992. Print.

Ross, Robert. L. "Cracking India: A Feminine View of Partition" *The Novels of Bapsi Sidhwa. ed.* R. K. Dhawan and Novi Kapadia. New Delhi: Prestige Books. 1996. Print.

Studlar, Gaylyn. " Masochism and Perverse Pleasure of the Cinema."*Film Theory and Criticism.*Ed. Gerald Mast, Marshall Cohen, Leo Braudy. 4th Ed. New York: Oxford University Press. 1992. Print.

Trurken, Marita, and Lisa Cartwright.*Practices of Looking: Practices of Looking: an Introduction to Visual Culture.* 3rdEd. New York: Oxford University Press, 2009. Print.

Wells, Paul. "Thou Art Translated: Analysing Animated Adaptation." *Adaptations: From Text to Screen Screen to Text. Ed.* Cartmell Deborah, Imelda Whelehan. New York: Routledge Taylor & Francis, 1999. Print.

Articles in Journals

Bhattacharya, Malini. "The Hidden Violence of Faith: The Widows of Vrindaban." *Social Scientist.* 29. 1 (2001) 81.Web. 18 April, 2013. http://www.jjstor.org/stable/3518273

Burton, David F. "Fire, Water and the Goddess: The Films of Deepa Mehta and Satyajit Ray as Critique of Hindu Patriarchy." *Journal of Religion & Film* 17.2 (2013) Web. 21 May 2014. http://digitalcommos.unomaha.edu/jrf/vol17/iss2/3

Butalia, Urvashi. "Community, State and Gender: On Women's Agency Durin Partition". *Economic and Political Weekly.* 28.17 (1993): 12-24. Print.

Clark, C. Fiona. " Victims, Perpetrators or Actors? Gender, Armed Conflict and Political violence." *Zubaan.*(2005): Print.

Fung, Amy. "Deepa Mehta's Canadian, American, Indian Bollywood Musical: Showing Canadian Their Country in Bollywood/ Hollywood." *London Journal of Canadian Studies* 21 (2005/6): 80. Print.

Jasmine Yuen-Carrucan." Politics of DeepaMehat's Water." *Bright Light Film Journal.*1 April 2009. Web. 22 August 2015. http:/ /brightlightsfilm.com/politics-deepa-mehtas-water/ #.WEqfPbJ97IU

Kemp, Phillip. "Calm Without, Fire With in". *The Criterion.* 4 November 2015. Web.13 July 2016.http//:www. criterion. com/current/posts/2872-charulata-calm-without-fire with in.

Lesage, Julia. 'Feminism film criticism: theory and practice', *Women and Film.*5.6 (1974):13. Print.

Makhlknecht, Johannes. "The Hollywood Novelization: Film as Literature or Literature as Film Promotion." *Poetics Today* 33.2 (summer 2012): Web. 10 December 2015.

Mehta, Deepa. "Citizen-Film Maker of the World." Richard Phillip. *WSWS. 6 August* 1999. Web.2 Feb 2016. http:// www. wsws. org/ ar-ti-cles/ 1999/ aug1999/mehta-a06. shtml

Mulvey, Laura. "British Feminist Film Theory's Female Spectators: Presence and Absence," *Camera Obscura.* 20. 21 (1989): 1-69. Print.

Nijhawan, Amita. " Dawning the Flow: Deepa Mehta's Water." *M/CJournal* 9.4 (2006): 28May 2016. Web.22 July 2015. http:/ /journal.media-culture.org.au/0609/3-nijhawan.php

Ozan, Rengin. "Feminist Cinema as Counter Cinema: Is Feminist Cinema Counter Cinema?" *Journal of Communication and Media Technologies* 5.3 (2015): Web. 7 September 2015.

Patil, Sunil. "Feminine Approach in Bapsi Sidhwa's Novel." *Indian*

Streams Research Journal. 4. 2 (2014). Web.9 March 2014.

Place, Janey, and Burton Julianne."Feminist Film Criticism." *Movie* 22 (1976). Print. Journal

Rana, Jayant. "Performing Dissent: Rape Narratives in Manjula Padhmanabhan's Lights Out !" *The Criterion* 7.2 (April 2016): 038. Web.10 April 2016.

Sontag, Susan. "Film and Theatre." *The Tulane Drama Review* 11.1 (Autumn 1966): 24-37. Print. MIT Press DOI: 10.2307/1125262 http://www.jstor.org/stable

Turin, Maureen. 'Gentlemen consume blondes', *Wide Angle* 1. (1970): Web. 15 July 2014.

Magazines and News Papers:

Catasouls, Jannette. " Under the Heel of Britain and Thumb of Hindu Law in 'Water'." *The New York Times* [New York] 28 April 2008. Print.

Deshpande, Manish. "In the line of fire" The Indian Express. 13 December 1998.Web.12 March 2008.

Islam, Jessica, and AnweshaMamtaz. "Violence as a form of repression as well as a form of resistance through Bapsi Sidhwa's Ice-Candy-Man and Deepa Mehta's Earth: 1947." *Evening Sun.* 7 August 2016.

Joshua, Anita. "Water Trickles In." *The Hindu.*July 2, 2006.

Mc Dowell, Edwin. "One in fifty novels published in this country were optioned by Hollywood". *The York Times* 14 July 1985: 1. Print.

McGowan, Sharon. "Excerpts from a Master Class with Deepa Mehta." *In Women Filmmakers: Refocussing,* edited by Jacqueline Levintin, Judith Plessis, and Valerie Raoul. Vancouver: UBC Press, 2003. 290-291.Print.

Menon, Ritu, and Kamala Bhasin. "An Exchange of Women: Abduction, Forcible Recovery, Silence Tragic Irony of Partitions Unsung." *Out Look.* 28 May 1997. Special Issue

Partition.Web.http://outlookindia.com/magzine/sectins/book/24

Orme, Michael. "The Bookshelf and the Screen" *Illustrated London News*, CLXXXVI 10 March 1934. 29 March 2016. Web. 368.

Ranchan and Razdan,"The Serpent and the Rope, India Made Real," T*he Illustrated Weekly of India* 87 (March1966): 47 Print.

Internet Sources

Ahluwalia, Ron. "Planet Bollywood" http://data/data/com.android.browser/files//66.mht. 4 November 2015.

Blumefield, J. Warren."Hyper-Masculinity, Twin Peaks, and Gendered Violence" *Huffpost.*22 May 2015. [Updated 21 May.2016].15 October 2016.

Ebert, Roger. "Earth"HYPERLINK "http://en.wikipedia.org/wiki/Chicago_Sun-Times" \o "Chicago Sun-Times"*Chicago Sun-Times*. 15 October 1999. 9 December 2008.

Faiyas, Afreen. "BapsiSidhwa and Her Rebels in Water" *Muse India* 67 May-June (2016). Web.http://pakistanpaindabad.blogspot.com/2007/06/bapsi-sidhwa-i wrote-naturally about.html.

Fischer, Lucy. "Women and Film – Cinema and Media Studies."*Oxford Bibliographies Online.* 28 October 2011. 1 May 2015 http://www.oxfordbibliographies.com/view/document

Frederic, and Mary Ann Brussat. "Film Theory Before 1945". 29 October 2013. Web.1May 2016. http://www. oxford bibliographies. com.

Havan, Araz. "Books vs. Movies Adaptations: The Never Ending Debate". *Daily Collegian.* 12 March 2013. Web.9 July 2015. http://dailycollegian.com/2013/03/12/books-vs-movies-adaptations-the-never-ending-debate.

Holden, Stephen. "Earth: India Torn Apart, as a Child Sees it". New York Times. 19 September 1999. Web.9 December 2008 http://www.nytimes.com/library/film/091099-earth-film-review.html

Khalid, Amna. "Critical Discourse Analysis of Gender Inequality and Exploitation in Our Lady of Alice Bhatti." 19 July 2014. Web. 07 July 2015. http://amnakhalidraja.blogspot.in/2014/07/critical -discourse-analysis-of-gender.html.

Maria, X Liu. "Obstructing the Male Gaze – Dependent Culture". *Huffpost.*16 December 2014 [updated February 15, 2015]. Web.14 April 2016. http://www.huttingtonpost.com

Renee, V. "Cinema as Art: The Philosophy of Andrei Tarkovesky." *No Film School.*November 2014.Web.15 January 2015.http://www.nofilmschool.com>2014/01> cinema-as-art

Simandan, V.M. "Julia Kristeva's Concepts of Intertextuality." *Life Style Systems.* 29 December 2010. Web.14 April 2016. http://www.simandan.com/kristeva-concepts-of-intertextuality.

Wijesirwardena, Panini, and Parwini Zora." The Plight of Widows in India".*World Socialist Website.*15 May 2006. Web.21 October 2014. http://www.wsws.org>wate-m15

Interviews

Mehta, Deepa. Interview by Richard Phillip.*WSWS Interview.* 6 August 1999. http://www.wsws.org/articles/1999/meh-a06.shtml.

Sidhwa, Bapsi. "Bapsi Sidhwa on Growing Up in Pakistan, Writing and theFuture of the Parsi Community" Raju Moza. *Huffington Post.*Web. 27 July 2015. http://www. huffington post. in/raju-moza/interview-bapsi-sidhwa-on-b-7847946.html.

Sidhwa, Bapsi. "Points of Departure-International Writers on Writing and Politics".Cited in *Points of Departure –*